# Interview Exercises for the **Police Recruit Assessment Process**

# Interview Exercises for the **Police Recruit Assessment Process**

Richard Malthouse
Jodi Roffey-Barentsen

# Acknowledgements

The authors would like to thank the following for their assistance with this book.

Ian Anstiss, Emma Barnes, Djamel Benlakehal, Sam Bright, Simon Carson, Paminder Chaudri, Jennifer Clark, Kevin Day, Michael Havers, Kim Van Niekerk, Carly Sanderson, Sarah Skultety, Carolyn Studd, Karen Thorne and Yavor Zlatev.

First published in 2010 by Learning Matters Ltd

© 2010 Richard Malthouse and Jodi Roffey-Barentsen

*British Library Cataloguing in Publication Data*
A CIP record for this book is available from the British Library.

All characters, organisations and places mentioned in this publication are fictitious and any resemblance to real persons, living or dead, is purely coincidental.

ISBN: 978 1 84445 461 7

Cover design by Topics – The Creative Partnership
Text design by Code 5 Design Associates Ltd.
Project Management by Deer Park Productions, Tavistock
Typeset by Kelly Winter
Printed and bound in Great Britain by Bell & Bain Ltd, Glasgow

Learning Matters Ltd
33 Southernhay East
Exeter EX1 1NX
Tel: 01392 215560
info@learningmatters.co.uk
www.learningmatters.co.uk

**Mixed Sources**
Product group from well-managed forests and other controlled sources
www.fsc.org   Cert no. TT-COC-002769
© 1996 Forest Stewardship Council
FSC

# Contents

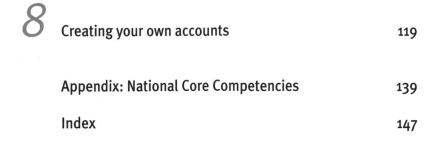

# Introduction

This chapter discusses the nature and purpose of a Competency Based Structured Interview (CBSI) and explains the interview process. It identifies the two types of questions you will be asked and considers the associated prompt questions.

The National Core Competencies are listed and you are given the opportunity to provide your own bulleted examples for each, based on your life experiences. Managing expectations and interview techniques are also explained, together with what to expect during the interview.

Two mnemonics are recommended to assist your understanding of the structure of the interview questions. A seven-step approach to preparing for the interview is explained and general advice is put forward in relation to the interview itself.

## The interview exercises

The interview exercises are formally referred to as a CBSI. Other terms you may have heard could include Structured Interviewing or Evidence Based Interviewing. Essentially, these types of interviews employ the same form of questioning techniques. They are used by many large organisations to make the interview process as fair as possible, as exactly the same questions are asked in every interview, using predetermined criteria. This means that one of the advantages of the CBSI is that any number of people can assess the candidates.

The criteria you will be assessed against are those contained within the National Core Competencies. These are shown in full in the Appendix and are discussed individually within the following chapters of this book.

## The interview process

Prior to the interviews you will be briefed as to which rooms are used and the general process of the CBSI. Following this you will be directed to a room where normally you will see just one person, the interviewer; this person will also assess your accounts. The interview will lack any small-talk or good-natured remarks you may be used to from typical job interviews. The interviewer will read you an explanation of the interview process. During the CBSI process:

- you will be asked four questions;
- for each question you will have a maximum of five minutes in which to answer;

- the interviewer will assess your account, marking as you speak;

- this person will time your account with a stop watch;

- water is provided.

Before each question is asked, the interviewer will explain to you which competencies are being assessed and a copy of the interview question will be given to you. This will assist you in case you forget what the original question was.

Time not used in your allocated five minutes for a question cannot be carried forward to use for another question. Further, if you finish your accounts very quickly then you will be asked to remain within the room until all the other candidates have also finished.

# About competency based structured interview questions

The questions you are asked are designed to draw from you an account of your life experiences and how you have interacted with other people. They are designed to discover how you have dealt with a situation in the past as it is likely that you will act in a similar way in the future. According to Reed (2009):

> The basic theory is that past behaviour in work related situations can be used as a predictor of future performance and studies have shown this technique to be about 5 times more accurate than traditional interview questions when selecting new employees.

(Reed, 2009, p3)

If you examine the National Core Competencies you will notice that they are all about people, how you interact with others, communicate with others, solve problems with other people and how you respect others' religions, lifestyles, views, etc. The questions are an opportunity for you to provide a specific account of your behaviour on one particular occasion and not a description of how you generally behave in various situations.

According to Cox (2007, p66), there are two common styles of questioning:

1. behavioural-based questions;

2. situational questions.

The first type asks you to *talk about the ways you have used your abilities in the past*. For example such a question will usually start with phrases like:

- *Tell me about a time when you. . .*

- *Give an example of an occasion where you. . .*

These are examples of the most common types of questions asked in competency based structured interviews, and are referred to as being behavioural based. You are being asked to draw upon your experience relevant to the question and describe, in detail, how you have behaved.

The other type of question described by Cox (2007, p66) *gives you a set of circumstances and asks you what you would do in that situation*. These are called situational questions. According to Lewis (2009, p1), these *are used as a tool to discover how your behaviour in a previous role or situation can contribute to your performance in the job being recruited for*. An example of such a question could be:

- *At work, a colleague makes a blatant racist statement to you. What will you do?*

Although the questions relate to the National Core Competencies, you are not assessed in terms of police-related experiences or behaviours. In other words, within the CBSI your account can be drawn from any situation such as school, home, work, a holiday, a club, voluntary work or any other social gathering. The questions are designed to assess your suitability to become a police officer in terms of your temperament, character and your general people skills.

## Prompts

Each question includes a number of prompts, designed to elicit further information from you. These are used if it appears that you have finished your account, and are designed to assist you – not to catch you out, trip you up or to challenge your account. If, for example, you were answering a question in relation to communication, the prompt question could be: *How did you know that you had been understood?* Don't be surprised if you feel that you have already alluded to this question. The interviewer will have about five or six prompt questions and these will be the same for each person. If the interviewer feels that the question has been fully met then she or he can choose not to use the prompt. If you are asked about something that you feel you have already referred to, it may be that you could add something to enable the interviewer to make more sense of what you are saying. The prompt questions may not fit your account perfectly but treat them as a gift and use them to enhance your account.

# The National Core Competencies

Lewis (2009) suggests that the word 'competency' is widely used in business environments and refers to the skills that are necessary to achieve an effective performance level in the job. In your interview you will be tested against the National Core Competencies and although each competency will be looked at in detail later in this book, it is beneficial to consider each in general terms. It is strongly recommended that you ensure that you are familiar with the National Core Competencies.

It is useful for you to consider how you have evidenced the competencies in some way. This is your opportunity to reflect on your life experiences and to focus on those experiences which best match the National Core Competencies. It may be that you have more than one experience that fits the competency. If this is the case, record them all. Noting them down as bullet points means that you can record the salient parts without writing too much. On the other hand, it may be that you realise that you have no experience or suitable examples for some of the competencies. That does not matter. What is important is that from this moment on you endeavour to do something about it to ensure you gain experience in that area. To do this you could volunteer for a job where your people skills will be utilised and tested. Remember, the competencies are all about dealing with people. You may not be tested on all of the competencies but it is recommended that you prepare for all seven.

The seven National Core Competencies are listed below and you are asked to provide an example which evidences your ability to match each competency.

The following competencies are reproduced in part with kind permission from *The Integrated Competency Behavioural Framework Version 9.0 (May 2007)* by Skills for Justice.

### 1. *Respect for race and diversity*

Considers and shows respect for the opinions, circumstances and feeling of colleagues and members of the public, no matter what their race, religion, position, background, circumstances, status or appearance.

Required level

- Understands other people's views and takes them into account.

- Is tactful and diplomatic when dealing with people.

- Treats them with dignity and respect at all times.

- Understands and is sensitive to social, cultural and racial differences.

---

**TASK 1**

Think about this competency and, drawing on your life experiences, consider when your behaviour has matched respect for race and diversity. You could take into account your experiences at work, social events, school, holidays, etc. Use the required level points to assist you. Bullet point your ideas below in very brief terms.

---

### 2. *Team working*

Develops strong working relationships inside and outside the team to achieve common goals. Breaks down barriers between groups and involves others in discussions and decisions.

Required level

- Works effectively as a team member and helps build relationships within it.

- Actively helps and supports others to achieve team goals.

---

**TASK 2**

Again think about this competency and consider when your behaviour has matched the National Core Competency team working. You could consider sport, voluntary work, a project at work, an expedition, etc. Use the required level points to assist you. Bullet point your ideas below.

---

### 3. Community and customer focus

Focuses on the customer and provides a high-quality service that is tailored to meet their individual needs. Understands the communities that are served and shows an active commitment to policing that reflects their needs and concerns.

Required level

- Provides a high level of service to customers.

- Maintains contact with customers, works out what they need and responds to them.

---

**TASK 3**

With this competency consider when your behaviour has matched community and customer focus. You could consider drawing on your experiences at work, voluntary situations, religious arenas, etc. Use the required level points to assist you. Bullet point your ideas below.

---

### 4. Effective communication

Communicates ideas and information effectively, both verbally and in writing. Uses language and a style of communication that is appropriate to the situation and people being addressed. Makes sure others understand what is going on.

Required level

- Communicates all needs, instructions and decisions clearly.

- Adapts the style of communication to meet the needs of the audience.

- Checks for understanding.

---

**TASK 4**

Consider when your behaviour has matched effective communication. Think about a time perhaps when you had difficulties communicating with another person or a group of people. Use the required level points to assist you. Bullet point your ideas below:

---

## 5. Problem solving

Gathers information from a range of sources. Analyses information to identify problems and issues and makes effective decisions.

Required level

- Gathers enough relevant information to understand specific issues and events.

- Uses information to identify problems and draw conclusions.

- Makes good decisions.

---

**TASK 5**

Consider when your behaviour has matched problem solving. This can be at work, a hobby or even a family event. It must be something to do with people and not working out how to repair a computer, etc. Use the required level points to assist you. Bullet point your ideas below.

---

## 6. Personal responsibility

Takes personal responsibility for making things happen and achieving results. Displays motivation, commitment, perseverance and conscientiousness. Acts with a high degree of integrity.

Required level

- Takes personal responsibility for own actions and for sorting out issues or problems that arise.

- Is focused on achieving results to required standards and developing skills and knowledge.

---

**TASK 6**

Consider when your behaviour has matched personal responsibility. Problem-solving may be worth considering where your actions have played a significant part in resolving an issue. Remember you are not being expected to achieve world peace; the issue can be very minor. Use the required level points to assist you. Bullet point your ideas below.

---

## 7. Resilience

Shows resilience, even in difficult circumstances. Prepared to make difficult decisions and has the confidence to see them through.

Required level

- Shows reliability and resilience in difficult circumstances.

- Remains calm and confident and responds logically and decisively in difficult situations.

---

**TASK 7**

Consider when your behaviour has matched resilience. Examples of resilience can mean doing the right thing when all around you disagree, or embarking on a course of action that is not popular but, nevertheless, necessary. Use the required level points to assist you. Bullet point your ideas below.

---

You should now have seven or more bulleted examples. At this stage they may be only general ideas but this is a good thing because it means that you have made a start in thinking about your own experiences. Some people find this stage difficult because they do not make the link between what they have done and the competencies. As explained earlier, the examples you choose do not have to be fantastic, the assessment process is not looking for people who have invented a ground-breaking medicine or heroically saved numerous lives. They are looking for people who can exhibit the competencies and the examples can be apparently unimportant events. However, it is not what you have done that matters, it is how you did it that is important.

Later we return to these examples and work on them to ensure they are suitable for the assessment centre by considering the positive and negative indicators.

# Managing your expectations

Do not expect this interview to be like any other job interview. As previously stated, there will be no small-talk. The interaction with the interviewer will be minimal. In fact, when you are answering the questions, do not be surprised if the interviewer does not even look at you. This apparent lack of interaction is there to ensure complete fairness. It is possible to encourage a candidate with non-verbal communication alone. The normal nodding of the head, a look of approval, a knowing raising of the eyebrows, etc., can all lead to a candidate feeling comfortable. However, it is unlikely that each of the interviewers would offer the same types and amount of non-verbal encouragement to all candidates. Therefore the interviewers do not interact with the candidates. For some candidates this has a profound effect because, culturally, non-participation by the listener in a conversation can be interpreted as them not being interested. As a result, and often unconsciously, some candidates withdraw from the conversation. This can be by not embellishing the account with suitable descriptions or detail, or simply ending the account before the five minutes are over. A suitable coping strategy can be to imagine that just over the shoulder of the interviewer is a friend or member of your family who is interested in hearing about your experiences. You can pretend to talk to them if it helps you to focus.

On occasion, there may be another person in the room. Don't be put off by this, as the reasons will be explained to you. Generally the reason is to ensure standardisation. As you give your account the interviewer will be assessing what you are saying against the criteria. A uniform approach to marking is essential; the interviewers are well trained and consistency in marking is maintained by their viewing each other during the assessment process.

# Interview techniques

Rather than thinking about the CBSI as an interview, it is helpful to consider it in terms of a presentation. You are given five minutes in which to speak on a question based on one of the competencies. Because you are aware of this you can prepare in advance. The caveat here is that if you only have one prepared answer for each competency then you cannot guarantee that what you have prepared will actually answer the question. Because of this it is recommended that you have at least three examples for each competency. As mentioned earlier, you will be asked a total of four questions. On occasion it could happen that an account you had prepared for, for instance, 'effective communication' is more appropriate as a response to the question you have been asked on 'respect for race and diversity'. Having three examples for each competency will mean that you have a total of 21 examples, so you can afford to mix and match.

## Answering competency based structured interview questions

According to Lewis (2009), when answering CBSI questions choose examples that are based on real experiences you have had and avoid the temptation to invent or embellish.

> *Your response needs to be relevant and sufficiently detailed to show that you understand what is required, that you possess the relevant core competency and can use it effectively.*
>
> (Lewis, 2009, p1)

This is easier than you may at first think. The Appendix identifies the positive and negative indicators for each competency. In other words, you are told exactly what is required of you and what is not; the indicators can be seen as the set criteria for the competency. Your account will be scored against these criteria so it should aim to reflect these. However, you also need to ensure that your account does not become a contrived attempt to include all the positive indicators (criteria). The quality of your account will depend on your preparation, hence the need to work on your examples beforehand.

The purpose of the interview is for you to show that you have met the necessary criteria. The emphasis is on you. On occasion, for instance when referring to the Team working competency, candidates forget about themselves by referring to 'we' and not 'I'. Remember the importance of 'me, myself and I'. Reed (2009, p3) offers the following advice:

- *describe the situation or problem;*
- *talk about the part YOU played in discovering the problem;*
- *describe what YOU did to resolve it, the actions YOU took;*
- *detail the successful result and use figures to illustrate.*

To this you can add:

- listen to the question asked;
- answer the question, not another you wished had been asked;
- remember the importance of me, myself and I.

## Structure

When speaking for five minutes on a subject it can be easy to forget where exactly you have got to, losing the main theme of your account. It is therefore helpful to structure your answer. A most effective mnemonic to help with this is SARA:

**S**   Situation

**A**   Action

**R**   Result

**A**   Analysis

> (Re-created with kind permission of The Interview Success Company Ltd, 2009)

### Situation

- What was the situation?
- Describe in detail
  - the place
  - time of day
  - location
  - who you were with
  - why you were there
  - the occasion
- What happened exactly?

### Action

- What action did you take?
- As a result of the situation, what did you do specifically?
- Why did you take that course of action?
- What else did you consider?
- Why did you not do that?

### Result

- What happened as a result of your action?
- What effect did your action have on the situation?
- What was:
  - said
  - heard
  - felt
  - changed, etc?

### Analysis

- Thinking about the situation and your actions at the time, what did you learn?
- What will you do differently next time?

Using the mnemonic SARA will help you account for your actions in a structured manner. If you consider all the points indicated above, then you will be able to relate your situation without repetition, straying from the point or running out of things to say.

You should aim to engage the interviewer by making your account tell a story. Many candidates begin their account by forgetting some small but important facts. For example, explaining:

- a little about the reasons for being at a place;

- who they were with;

- why they were with the person;

- the geographic nature of the place if relevant;

- the time of day;

- underlying or ongoing problems.

For the interviewer to be able to make full sense of your account, you will need to explain some of the elements that may easily be taken for granted. For you, these facts may be completely obvious, for the listener however, they need explaining. Remember, the interviewer does not know anything about you, your background or the situation you are describing. Therefore be very explicit and clear in your account.

An alternative to the SARA mnemonic is the R-SARA method:

**R**    Result for impact

**S**    Situation

**A**    Action

**R**    Result (explained)

**A**    Analysis

The additional 'Result for impact' category is used to get the attention of the listener. Normally this will take the form of just one line or statement. For example:

> *When working at the local supermarket I reduced sickness by 65% by introducing a new work roster.*

> *When working as a life guard at the local swimming pool I reduced the number of accidents by over 85% by introducing innovative safety measures.*

> *In my role as a Police Community Support Officer I prevented a racial incident at the local mosque.*

The later R – Result – can then be explained in detail at the appropriate place. You will notice that the R-SARA mnemonic is useful when describing an account within the problem-solving core competency.

# Preparing for your interview

Once you have found a suitable example for each of the seven core competencies using brief bullet points, you should consider the following seven steps in preparation for the interview.

## Step 1 Identify a question

There are only a certain number of questions that you can be asked and it is possible for you to predict them. For example, the competency in relation to Effective communication identifies the required level, which you can use as a starting point. For example:

*Communicates all needs, instructions and decisions clearly. Adapts the style of communication to meet the needs of the audience. Checks for understanding.*

Look at the required level above and ask yourself, if you were writing a question, what could it be?

Typically the type of questions could be like this:

*Give me an example of when you adapted your style of communication to meet the needs of another.*

*Tell me how you have checked a person has understood you.*

What you are doing is getting into the mind of the people who have written this exercise. As a result, your understanding of the process will increase. This leads to the next step.

## Step 2 Consider a suitable answer

Refer back to the seven tasks and your bullet points. For each of the competencies, think of a further two examples. As before, it is wise not to invent an example or exaggerate an existing one. Your life experiences should enable you to find examples for all of the competencies. Think about your answer and if you are happy with it go on to the next step.

## Step 3 Write the account in full

From the bullet points you can then enhance your account by writing it out in full. As you do this, use the SARA or R-SARA mnemonic as headings. This will ensure structure to your writing.

## Step 4 Compare and contrast

The next step is to compare your account to the positive indicators and ask yourself if it is likely to cover any of these. If it does not, then reconsider either the example you have chosen or the way in which you have written your account.

## Step 5 Rehearsal

Using the bullet points from step 2 and having added to them to reflect step 3, talk your account through. Just thinking it through is not sufficient. By actually talking through your account you will be using the part of the brain that deals with speech and not the part that deals with memory of sound. Do this for as many times as it takes to get through the account without forgetting what you wish to say. When you can do this without your bullet points, go to the next step.

## Step 6 Timings

Find a clock, watch or stop watch and either take a note of the time or set it to five minutes. Turn the clock away from you and begin to speak. When you have finished your account, look at the time and see how near the five minutes you are. If there is time remaining, consider adding material or speaking more slowly. Conversely, if you run over time consider removing some material or speaking more quickly.

## Step 7 Practise

No matter how well you think you know your accounts, it is imperative that you keep practising, ensuring smooth, logical, well-structured responses to the questions. However, it is highly likely that, due to nerves, you will speak at a quicker pace during the interview, so don't be too surprised if you have some time remaining.

On the other hand, if you find during the interview that you do not have enough time to finish your account, do not worry, as there are no marks allocated to finishing.

# The interview itself

During the interview you will be seated. Assume a position in which you will feel comfortable and yet professional. Tucking one foot under you is inappropriate, as is sitting slumped. Sit up, place your hands on your lap and pay attention to what is said to you. You will not be marked on appearance, but wearing smart clothes will make you feel more confident. Therefore, consider carefully what you are going to wear.

If for some reason you discover that you have missed out a large chunk of what you had prepared, don't worry about it; the only person who will be aware of this fact will be you. Ensure that you allude to the missing part by saying something like, *I'd also like to add that . . .* or *Going back to the beginning of my account I would like to add that. . .* You can go backwards and forwards in your account, just ensure the interviewer is aware of what you are doing.

Beware of the self-fulfilling prophesy: if you realise afterwards that you have made a mistake or that another example might have been more appropriate, do not worry about it or dwell on it. For some candidates it is natural to worry about their performance or feel disappointed with themselves if they have made a mistake. The problem with this is that thinking back to a problem may well affect what you are doing at the time and could distract you. So try to stay in the here and now, without worrying about what happened before.

On occasions candidates offer a full account that has nothing to do with the question asked. The reasons for this could be many, but discussions with prospective candidates suggest that they misinterpreted the question or felt that their prepared account was to be used come what may. Obviously this policy should be discouraged – only use an account if appropriate to do so.

---

**TASK 8**

Look at the following five accounts and decide which competency each best reflects. The answers are at the end of this chapter. (All accounts drawn upon within this book are based on accounts given by police assessment candidates.)

Account 1

Account 2

Account 3

Account 4

Account 5

Account 6

---

# Account 1

*I was called to one of the car parks at Heathrow. On arrival I spoke to one of the car park staff and they had said that the traffic was backed up on all levels. People were cutting across lanes and getting stuck. They had staff trying to sort it out but there weren't enough people and the drivers were starting to get aggravated as they had been waiting about 1½ hours. I said I would call more of my colleagues to help on other floors, whilst I took the top floor. I asked if it was possible to open the gates at the bottom to allow the traffic to flow out better, which they agreed to do.*

*I went to the top floor to help out the car park staff and was met with a group of people who were quite upset and wanted to know what was going on. I listened to their complaints and explained that it was just the sheer weight of traffic and that the barriers at the bottom had been opened so it shouldn't be too much longer. People were beeping their horns, which was making people even more agitated. I went along the line seeing if everything was OK and asked people who were beeping their horns not to do so as it was not helping the situation.*

*As I was walking up and down the queues I was asked what was going on by a woman in a car. As I looked into the car I could see the mother had a little baby. She was quite upset and frustrated and the baby was crying. She said that the baby needed feeding as she was expecting to be home by now. I asked if she had a bottle of milk, which she had so I offered to heat it up. I asked the car park staff if they had a kettle in their staff room to heat up the bottle. Once it was heated I took it back to the lady in the car but quickly checked on what was happening with the traffic situation to update the lady. I apologised for the problems caused but we were dealing with it as quickly as possible and that if she needed anything else that I would be around and just to ask.*

*I liaised with car park staff just in case they needed any other assistance anywhere else and if the deployment of people was working and moving the traffic on. I tried to sort the problem with the traffic as quickly as possible and to answer the drivers' concerns and update them on any progress.*

# Account 2

*Where I currently work, we are always having our cells damaged by prisoners scratching into the wall, floor and sometimes around or in the toilet. This problem was beginning to get out of hand because we could no longer establish what old graffiti was or what was new. We were all assigned tasks to do around the custody suite and the person who was given the task of taking on the criminal damage was struggling with it. I spoke to my supervising officer and stated that perhaps it was more suitable to share the work and I volunteered myself to help out.*

*Since joining my colleague in the battle against the criminal damage, we have managed to photograph all of the cells and record any historic damage. We have a folder out in the office which any colleagues can refer to should any damage become present in the cells. This can also save us a lot of time owing to the fact that we now no longer have to download the CCTV from the cell to see if the previous occupier was the culprit.*

# Account 3

*When I was a volunteer at a special needs school I often had to supervise a class of 12 or more children with learning disabilities on a daily basis. My task was to look after the class when the teacher was not around and to make sure everyone and everything was OK and the children's health and safety were observed. The task was mundane but was a very important one at the same time – some of the children had severe disabilities and communication was difficult with them and there were no teachers around as they were busy with other children.*

*I stayed focused on the task by trying to adapt my communication to the children and to explain things they should and should not do in the classroom. Sometimes I had to repeat myself or use hand gestures to those who could not understand what I was trying to say to them. For one or two of the children I had to draw pictures on the board to explain exactly what I meant.*

*Although it was difficult at times to communicate with some of the children in the classroom I ensured that no one was feeling unhappy and everyone was safe – I was talking to them, asking questions, involving them in conversations.*

*I felt happy that I achieved my task and I was congratulated by the headmaster and the teachers for my good work and they praised my work as a volunteer.*

# Account 4

*In a GP's practice where I used to work we were given targets by the government called Quality and outcomes. In order to help us achieve this, receptionists were given administrative work to do toward these, which included organising appointments and checkups.*

*Last year I was not assigned any work to do towards these targets as I had taken on other work elsewhere. From looking at target figures for a set month, which I checked regularly to keep up to date on how the surgery was doing, I noticed that one target was quite low. After checking the work lists, I noticed that the target was not assigned to anyone. I notified management and offered to take responsibility for organising the achievement of this target, as I knew other receptionists had a lot of other responsibilities and a large workload. I hadn't done the targets for this area before so I spoke to members of staff so I could gain some knowledge to help me organise the best way to approach the work.*

*I fitted this work into my normal workload but made sure the extra work would not affect it. I checked with management and doctors that I was doing the work correctly as I did not want to miss anything or get anything wrong. The work I needed to do was quite repetitive, going through lists and lists of people's names. I worked out a way of breaking it down to keep my attention and to make sure I did not miss anything.*

*We had deadlines in order to reach our set targets so I did audits regularly to help me prioritise my work and to make sure I would reach the target in time. If I didn't, the surgery could miss out on valuable money and I feel I would have let my colleagues down.*

# Account 5

*I work as a volunteer family support worker with Youth Support. On many occasions I deal with both adults and children who are angry or upset or finding it difficult to understand the behaviour of others. I was working for several months with an 11-year-old girl who had learning difficulties. She had suffered the bereavement of her mother and was an only child to her father. She was having problems in school due to lack of self-confidence and was consequently being bullied. She had very quickly formed a close attachment to me but I had to tell her that the one-to-one sessions with me were coming to an end.*

*I chose a time (after a telephone discussion with her father) when she would feel at her best, and a place where she would be relaxed and able to focus properly on what I was saying without distractions. I explained to her how well she had done on the programme and that this meant we had achieved our goal. I kept my vocabulary at a level she was able to understand and because of the setting she was able to ask me questions and feel that I was not in any hurry to leave. It was quiet so I was able to hear everything she said and listen properly to her.*

*I gave her a diary of all our outings with details and pictures of places we had visited. I focused on the positive outcome of her time with me – that her self-esteem was high, she had gone on to a new school and had a new set of friends – and that if she experienced any further difficulties she could contact the organisation and someone would be able to advise her even if it was not me.*

*I suggested she choose what she would like to do for our last two outings and instead of making these weekly, as they had been, I arranged for them to be fortnightly, thus giving her time to adjust to the finish of the programme. This would also enable her to ask any further questions that she might have about the work we had done together or her future.*

*I made sure that at all times I treated her with dignity and respect. I was confident that she had understood everything I said; that she had everything in writing to refer to, and that I had listened carefully to all her comments and answered all her questions.*

You notice that the accounts can be used for more than one of the core competencies; it is just a matter of how you subsequently write it up.

# Ten tips for answering competency based structured interview questions

1. Familiarise yourself with the National Core Competencies.

2. Use the seven-step process to develop suitable accounts.

3. Develop 21 accounts for the CBSI.

4. Structure your examples with SARA or R-SARA.

5. Practise your accounts.

6. Dress smartly.

7. Sit appropriately.

8. Listen to the question being asked.

9. Answer the question, not another you wished had been asked.

10. Remember the importance of 'me, myself and I'.

# Summary

In this section we have:

- discussed the nature and purpose of a Competency Based Structured Interview and considered the interview process;

- identified the two types of questions you may be asked and the associated prompt questions;

- listed the National Core Competencies and encouraged bulleted examples for each;

- explained what to expect during the interview;

- offered the mnemonics SARA and R-SARA to structure interview responses;

- provided a seven-step approach to preparing for the interview;

- linked actual accounts to the core competencies.

The following chapters will guide you through the seven-step process for each of the seven National Core Competencies.

# Suggested answers

Account 1. This could cover Problem solving, Community and customer focus or Personal responsibility.

Account 2. Problem solving, Personal responsibility and, if written up in the right way, Team working.

Account 3. Respect for race and diversity and Problem solving.

Account 4. Problem-solving, Team working or Personal responsibility.

Account 5. Respect for race and diversity, Community and customer focus, Effective Communication or Resilience.

# References

Cox, P (2007) *Passing the Police Recruit Assessment Process*. Exeter: Learning Matters

Lewis, A (2009) Competency Based Interview Questions Made Easy. Blue Sky Interviews. **www.blueskyinterviews.co.uk/int_art10.htm** 22 August 2009

Reed, A (2009) Competency Based Interview Questions Made Easy. Blue Sky Interviews. **www.blueskyinterviews.co.uk/int_art02.htm** 22 August 2009

The Interview Success Company Ltd (2009) Course material SARA

# Further reading

Malthouse, R and Roffey-Barentsen, J (2009) *Written Exercises for the Police Recruit Assessment Process*. Exeter: Learning Matters

Malthouse, R., Kennard, P and Roffey-Barentsen, J (2009) *Interactive Exercises for the Police Recruit Assessment Process. Succeeding at Role Plays*. Exeter: Learning Matters

# Useful websites

**www.learningmatters.co.uk** Offers various police and law-related publications.

**www.theinterviewsuccesscompany.co.uk** Offers guidance in relation to passing the assessment centre process and further training.

# Chapter 1
## Respect for race and diversity

## Introduction

This chapter concentrates on the National Core Competency Respect for race and diversity, identifying the required level for the competency as well as the positive and negative indicators. It discusses a number of accounts candidates have used during their interviews as examples. You are invited to identify which of the positive indicators are evident in the accounts and how they could be improved.

The competency Respect for race and diversity is defined below.

*1. Respect for race and diversity.*
*Considers and shows respect for the opinions, circumstances and feeling of colleagues and members of the public, no matter what their race, religion, position, background, circumstances, status or appearance.*

The required level, which is *a further statement describing the required standard for that competency* (Cox, 2007, p8), is indicated here.

*Required level*
*Understands other people's views and takes them into account. Is tactful and diplomatic when dealing with people. Treats them with dignity and respect at all times. Understands and is sensitive to social, cultural and racial differences.*

Further to the above are the positive indicators. These are a list of the behaviours that you will be expected to demonstrate during the assessment centre process (they have also been previously referred to as 'criteria'). During the assessment centre process you will be tested three times on each of the competencies. This means that you do not have to ensure that each of the positive indicators is addressed in every account. Further, although the indicators are considered during the interview, they also apply to other parts of the assessment centre process such as the interactive exercises and the written test.

## Positive indicators

- Sees issues from other people's viewpoints.
- Is polite, tolerant and patient with people inside and outside the organisation, treating them with respect and dignity.

- Respects the needs of everyone involved when sorting out disagreements.

- Shows understanding and sensitivity to people's problems and vulnerabilities.

- Deals with diversity issues and gives positive practical support to staff who may feel vulnerable.

- Listens to and values others' views and opinions.

- Uses language in an appropriate way and is sensitive to the way it may affect people.

- Acknowledges and respects a broad range of social and cultural customs and beliefs and values within the law.

- Understands what offends others and adapts own actions accordingly.

- Respects and maintains confidentiality, where appropriate.

- Delivers difficult messages sensitively.

- Challenges attitudes and behaviour which are abusive, aggressive or discriminatory.

- Takes into account others' personal needs and interests.

- Supports minority groups both inside and outside their organisation.

## Negative indicators

A list of negative indicators identifies behaviour which is not wanted; this is listed below. Read through the list and ask yourself if at any time you have exhibited any of these traits. Don't worry, it does not mean that you are considered a racist if you have. The purpose of this exercise is to raise your awareness of the topic.

- Does not consider other people's feelings.

- Does not encourage people to talk about personal issues.

- Criticises people without considering their feelings and motivation.

- Makes situations worse with inappropriate remarks, language or behaviour.

- Is thoughtless and tactless when dealing with people.

- Is dismissive and impatient with people.

- Does not respect confidentiality.

- Unnecessarily emphasises power and control in situations where this is not appropriate.

- Intimidates others in an aggressive and overpowering way.

- Uses humour inappropriately.

- Shows bias and prejudice when dealing with people.

You may have exhibited some of the negative indicators at some stage. Now that you are aware of these you are in a position to ensure that in your day-to-day activities you can address any such habits. Of these, perhaps the most common is that of using humour inappropriately.

It is good practice to read through the negative indicators as they indicate exactly what you must not do. By changing the negative indicator to a positive statement you will ensure you are doing things in the correct way. For instance, negative indicator 'does not consider other people's feelings', can be changed to 'does consider other people's feelings', which can be evidenced in your account.

---

**TASK 1**

Consider the following: if you are sent an inappropriate or racist email, what are you going to do – forward it to your friends or delete it immediately?

Remember that within this competency you are considering both race and diversity. According to Malthouse, Kennard and Roffey-Barentsen (2009), *Diversity is described under six strands, namely*:

1. *Race*

2. *Gender*

3. *Disability*

4. *Sexual orientation*

5. *Age*

6. *Religion*

---

*Considerations of diversity go beyond the legislation; having respect for diversity means accepting that not everyone is just like you. It means taking time and effort to consider what life is like for others. In general terms it means treating other people as you would like to be treated yourself.*

(Malthouse, Kennard and Roffey-Barentsen, 2009, p12)

Unlike the other competencies, if you fail this competency at any stage with a D grade, then you will fail the whole of the assessment process no matter how well you may have done in the other assessment activities.

## Account examples

The candidates were asked to:

*Tell me about an occasion when you have had to consider something from another person's point of view.*

**TASK 2**

Consider the following three accounts and:

(a)  Identify which of the positive indicators are demonstrated in each account.

(b)  Think about how each could be improved.

(c)  Note any other general observations you may have.

The positive indicators have been reproduced at the end of each account for your use and there is space for general observations.

Suggested answers are provided at the end of the chapter. However, do be aware that here you are only assessing the written word and not a person in an interview situation.

# Account 1

*My wife and I are from different religions, my wife is a devout Christian, while I am a Muslim, we were raised with different beliefs and culture. Although before getting married we discussed many important issues, we only briefly discussed religious festivals such as Christmas.*

*I remember our first Christmas together, and when my wife wanted a Christmas tree in the house it became an issue as I had never celebrated Christmas before, and I always thought Christmas was only exchanging cards.*

*I decided to find out more about Christmas and what it means to a Christian. I talked to my wife in a sensitive manner, and listened to her and considered her feelings, I also saw the issue from her point of view and showed her tolerance and patience.*

*I also spoke to our local vicar and asked him to explain it more to me, and this enabled me to understand the commitment of my wife to Christmas. It is important that beliefs do not get in the way of living happily, I adapted to her beliefs by learning and respecting her religion.*

| Positive indicators | Yes |
|---|---|
| Sees issues from other people's viewpoints. | |
| Is polite, tolerant and patient with people inside and outside the organisation, treating them with respect and dignity. | |
| Respects the needs of everyone involved when sorting out disagreements. | |
| Shows understanding and sensitivity to people's problems and vulnerabilities. | |
| Deals with diversity issues and gives positive practical support to staff who may feel vulnerable. | |
| Listens to and values others' views and opinions. | |
| Uses language in an appropriate way and is sensitive to the way it may affect people. | |
| Acknowledges and respects a broad range of social and cultural customs and beliefs and values within the law. | |

Understands what offends others and adapts own actions accordingly.

Respects and maintains confidentiality, where appropriate.

Delivers difficult messages sensitively.

Challenges attitudes and behaviour which are abusive, aggressive or discriminatory.

Takes into account others' personal needs and interests.

Supports minority groups both inside and outside their organisation.

*General observations*

# Account 2

*This situation occurred while I was working as a Safer Transport Police Community Support Officer. My job involved travelling on the buses throughout the borough, preventing anti-social behaviour and criminal damage and generally making everyone's journey safer. When the role was first created, it was obvious that there were many problems and my time was taken up with youth disorder and general anti-social behaviour including fare evasion.*

*After a couple of months, most passengers were aware of who the Safer Transport Team were and why we were travelling on the buses. However, after a while, I began to notice just how hard a journey could be for the elderly passengers. For example, someone with a walking stick, or even in a wheelchair. I could see how uncomfortable they looked while travelling on a bus full of schoolchildren and it was surprising just how many elderly fell over on buses just because they are not as agile as younger people.*

*One day on returning to the police station, I was speaking to my sergeant about the situation, and he asked if I had any ideas. I knew that I could speak to individual people on the buses, but I wanted to contact larger groups. I suggested that I could visit sheltered housing accommodation in the borough and talk to the residents about the role of the Safer Transport Team. I contacted the local council and they sent me a list of sheltered accommodation in the area. There were at least 50 different homes. I sent a letter to each housing manager and soon had some meetings arranged.*

*When I visit the elderly, I talk about the role of the Safer Transport Team and then ask if they have any questions or more importantly any concerns that they have while travelling on the buses. I make a note of any issues and tell the residents that I will pass on any comments to my sergeant who in turn will discuss the problems with Transport for London.*

*It was clear that the elderly have many worries and difficulties while travelling on public transport and it can be a very daunting task getting from a to b. Having now attended quite a few meetings, I enjoy talking with the elderly and being able to help and reassure them.*

**Positive indicators**                                    **Yes**

Sees issues from other people's viewpoints.

Is polite, tolerant and patient with people inside and outside the organisation, treating them with respect and dignity.

Respects the needs of everyone involved when sorting out disagreements.

Shows understanding and sensitivity to people's problems and vulnerabilities.

Deals with diversity issues and gives positive practical support to staff who may feel vulnerable.

Listens to and values others' views and opinions.

Uses language in an appropriate way and is sensitive to the way it may affect people.

Acknowledges and respects a broad range of social and cultural customs and beliefs and values within the law.

Understands what offends others and adapts own actions accordingly.

Respects and maintains confidentiality, where appropriate.

Delivers difficult messages sensitively.

Challenges attitudes and behaviour which are abusive, aggressive or discriminatory.

Takes into account others' personal needs and interests.

Supports minority groups both inside and outside their organisation.

*General observations*

# Account 3

*I had a situation in the store where I worked when three customers complained about a group of children who were shouting and using abusive language inside and outside the store. The customers were clearly very unhappy and said they felt intimidated and not safe while shopping. They told me that as regular customers they don't deserve to be treated in this way and they made it clear unless something is done immediately they will consider going somewhere else to shop.*

*I spoke to the customers concerned and assured them that I as a store security and customer service officer will do my best to sort it out – I have raised the issue to the store manager, informed the town CCTV room and the police as well as recorded it in my book. I also went to speak to the children and I have tried to understand the situation from each point of view, without jumping to conclusions, trying to gather as much information as possible. I have also informed the local town council about the problem.*

*As a result the children got a new, open, safe playground and when the customers returned they were happy to see no kids shouting or swearing. They said they are grateful to everyone who made them feel safer and confident in the store. I was very happy to see them again and that the children have finally found a safer and better place to go and things to do without obstructing customers and abusing them. The three customers went to the manager and thanked for the help.*

*I think if I hadn't acted as I did, these customers would never come back for shopping and the children would continue to behave as they did, as well as the latter might get in more trouble, including with the Police. The problem would probably grow – the store would lose customers and would receive complaints from everywhere. It was the right thing to do and important to identify the problem, to make the right decision at the time and to inform the authorities and the management.*

**Positive indicators**                                 **Yes**

Sees issues from other people's viewpoints.

Is polite, tolerant and patient with people inside and outside the organisation, treating them with respect and dignity.

Respects the needs of everyone involved when sorting out disagreements.

Shows understanding and sensitivity to people's problems and vulnerabilities.

Deals with diversity issues and gives positive practical support to staff who may feel vulnerable.

Listens to and values others' views and opinions

Uses language in an appropriate way and is sensitive to the way it may affect people.

Acknowledges and respects a broad range of social and cultural customs and beliefs and values within the law.

Understands what offends others and adapts own actions accordingly.

Respects and maintains confidentiality, where appropriate.

Delivers difficult messages sensitively.

Challenges attitudes and behaviour which are abusive, aggressive or discriminatory.

Takes into account others' personal needs and interests

Supports minority groups both inside and outside their organisation

*General observations*

## Account 1 discussion

| **Positive indicators** | **Yes** |
|---|---|
| Sees issues from other people's viewpoints. | ✓ |
| Is polite, tolerant and patient with people inside and outside the organisation, treating them with respect and dignity. | ✓ |
| Respects the needs of everyone involved when sorting out disagreements. | |
| Shows understanding and sensitivity to people's problems and vulnerabilities. | ✓ |
| Deals with diversity issues and gives positive practical support to staff who may feel vulnerable. | |
| Listens to and values others' views and opinions | ✓ |
| Uses language in an appropriate way and is sensitive to the way it may affect people. | ✓ |
| Acknowledges and respects a broad range of social and cultural customs and beliefs and values within the law. | ✓ |
| Understands what offends others and adapts own actions accordingly. | |
| Respects and maintains confidentiality, where appropriate. | |
| Delivers difficult messages sensitively. | |
| Challenges attitudes and behaviour which are abusive, aggressive or discriminatory. | |
| Takes into account others' personal needs and interests | ✓ |
| Supports minority groups both inside and outside their organisation | |

### *General observations*

1.  This is a very strong example drawing upon experiences from the home, which is quite acceptable.

2.  This would benefit from further structure (SARA).

3.  More positive indicators might have been ticked had the account been longer. This means that the candidate can afford to go into greater detail in some areas; SARA would assist this.

4.  The reference to *sensitive manner* leads the marker to the competency 'Shows understanding and sensitivity to people's problems and vulnerabilities' without being a direct copy of the competency.

## Account 2 discussion

| Positive indicators | Yes |
| --- | --- |
| Sees issues from other people's viewpoints. | ✓ |
| Is polite, tolerant and patient with people inside and outside the organisation, treating them with respect and dignity. | ✓ |
| Respects the needs of everyone involved when sorting out disagreements. | |
| Shows understanding and sensitivity to people's problems and vulnerabilities. | ✓ |
| Deals with diversity issues and gives positive practical support to staff who may feel vulnerable. | |
| Listens to and values others' views and opinions. | ✓ |
| Uses language in an appropriate way and is sensitive to the way it may affect people. | |
| Acknowledges and respects a broad range of social and cultural customs and beliefs and values within the law. | |
| Understands what offends others and adapts own actions accordingly. | |
| Respects and maintains confidentiality, where appropriate. | |
| Delivers difficult messages sensitively. | |
| Challenges attitudes and behaviour which are abusive, aggressive or discriminatory. | |
| Takes into account others' personal needs and interests. | |
| Supports minority groups both inside and outside their organisation. | ✓ |

### *General observations*
1.  In general this is an appropriate account, it answers the question and is well considered.

2.  This would benefit from a little more structure, e.g. SARA.

3.  The issue of age discrimination has been considered here and not the more obvious race/sexual equality.

## Account 3 discussion

| Positive indicators | Yes |
|---|---|
| Sees issues from other people's viewpoints. | ✓ |
| Is polite, tolerant and patient with people inside and outside the organisation, treating them with respect and dignity. | ✓ |
| Respects the needs of everyone involved when sorting out disagreements. | ✓ |
| Shows understanding and sensitivity to people's problems and vulnerabilities. | ✓ |
| Deals with diversity issues and gives positive practical support to staff who may feel vulnerable. | |
| Listens to and values others' views and opinions. | ✓ |
| Uses language in an appropriate way and is sensitive to the way it may affect people. | |
| Acknowledges and respects a broad range of social and cultural customs and beliefs and values within the law. | |
| Understands what offends others and adapts own actions accordingly. | |
| Respects and maintains confidentiality, where appropriate. | |
| Delivers difficult messages sensitively. | |
| Challenges attitudes and behaviour which are abusive, aggressive or discriminatory. | ✓ |
| Takes into account others' personal needs and interests. | ✓ |
| Supports minority groups both inside and outside their organisation. | ✓ |

### *General observations*

1. This has scored well due to the fact that it considers the topic from a number of perspectives.

2. It is not judgemental.

3. This includes the SARA mnemonic which will benefit the candidate during the interview itself.

4. The 'Situation' element of SARA would benefit from an explanation that the candidate was a security guard: it assists to paint the picture.

# Summary

You have seen how others have prepared for their interview and hopefully you can learn from these examples. It is not just a case of regurgitating the positive indicators and expecting a high mark. A structured approach to a well thought-out account of an appropriate experience takes time to prepare. Often it is not until you think carefully about your experience that you realise it may be appropriate for inclusion. Some of these accounts began as a couple of bullet points and were then worked upon. It is helpful to use what is known as the 'exhaustive whys'. According to Roffey-Barentsen and Malthouse (2009, p.33), *A useful technique here is to ask as many 'whys' as you can about the situation*. For example:

> *The children are swearing at the shoppers. Why? They enjoy it. Why? Because they are bored. Why? Because they have nothing to do. Why? Because there are no facilities for them. Why? Because no one has done anything about it. Why? . . . I don't know.*

When you exhaust the whys you arrive at an improved understanding of a situation and are better placed to do something about it from an informed view. Your next move is to discuss the situation with others to gain a balanced perspective. What the candidate in the third account did not do was to assume guilt on the part of the children, who had admittedly been behaving badly. Maintaining a neutral position is appropriate within the arena of race and diversity. The role of the police officer is not to judge but to investigate.

# References

Cox, P (2007) *Passing the Police Recruit Assessment Process*. Exeter: Learning Matters

Malthouse, R, Kennard, P and Roffey-Barentsen, J (2009) *Interactive Exercises for the Police Recruit Assessment Process. Succeeding at Role Plays*. Exeter: Learning Matters

Roffey-Barentsen, J and Malthouse, R (2009) *Reflective Practice in the Lifelong Learning Sector.* Exeter: Learning Matters

# *Chapter 2*
# Team working

## Introduction

This chapter concentrates on the National Core Competency Team working, identifying the required level for the competency as well as the positive and negative indicators. Next, it discusses a number of accounts candidates have used during their interviews as examples. You are invited to identify which of the positive indicators are evident in the accounts and how they could be improved. Further, it discusses the appropriateness of weaving the language used in the competencies and positive indicators into your own accounts.

The competency Team working is defined below.

*2. Team working*
*Develops strong working relationships inside and outside the team to achieve common goals. Breaks down barriers between groups and involves others in discussions and decisions.*

The required level is as follows.

*Required level*
*Works effectively as a team member and helps build relationships within it. Actively helps and supports others to achieve team goals.*

Further to the above are the positive indicators. These are a list of the behaviours that you will be expected to demonstrate during the assessment centre process (they have also been previously referred to as 'criteria'). During the assessment centre process you will be tested three times on each of the competencies. This means that you do not have to ensure that each of the positive indicators is addressed in every account. Further, although the indicators are considered during the interview, they also apply to other parts of the assessment centre process such as the interactive exercises and the written test.

## Positive indicators

- Understands own role in a team.
- Actively supports and assists the team to reach their objectives.
- Is approachable and friendly to others.

- Makes time to get to know people.

- Co-operates with and supports others.

- Offers to help other people.

- Asks for and accepts help when needed.

- Develops mutual trust and confidence in others.

- Willingly takes on unpopular or routine tasks.

- Contributes to team objectives no matter what the direct personal benefit may be.

- Acknowledges that there is often a need to be a member of more than one team.

- Takes pride in their team and promotes their team's performance to others.

## Negative indicators

A list of negative indicators identifies behaviour which is not wanted.

- Does not volunteer to help other team members.

- Is only interested in taking part in high-profile and interesting activities.

- Takes credit for success without recognising the contribution of others.

- Works to own agenda rather than contributing to team performance.

- Allows small exclusive groups of people to develop.

- Plays one person off against another.

- Restricts and controls what information is shared.

- Does not let people say what they think.

- Does not offer advice or get advice from others.

- Shows little interest in working jointly with other groups to meet the goals of everyone involved.

- Does not discourage conflict within the organisation.

It is good practice to read through the negative indicators as they indicate exactly what you must not do. By changing the negative indicator to a positive statement you will ensure you are doing things in the correct way. For instance, negative indicator 'does not volunteer to help other team members', can be changed to 'does volunteer to help other team members', which can be evidenced in your account.

# Account examples

The candidates were asked to:

*Tell me about a specific time when you have co-operated with others to achieve a goal or objective.*

---

**TASK 1**

Consider the following three accounts and:

(a) Identify which of the positive indicators are demonstrated in each account.

(b) Think about how each could be improved.

(c) Note any other general observations you may have.

The positive indicators have been reproduced at the end of each account for your use and there is space for general observations.

Suggested answers are provided at the end of the chapter. However do be aware that here you are only assessing the written word and not a person in an interview situation.

---

# Account 1

*I belong to a rock-climbing club called The Castle. They run rock-climbing holidays in Spain every year in summer. Last year a few friends and I decided to go on one of these holidays. There were ten of us all going together. We didn't all know each other but our aim was to climb together and enjoy the Spanish countryside. A lot of gear is required for outdoor rock climbing. We each had to bring a piece of equipment with us. I agreed to bring a 90m climbing rope which everyone would be using. More ropes would be provided by our club but we had to provide one ourselves. The rest of our team brought various other bits of equipment along too.*

*We travelled on the plane together. I made an effort to get to know everyone that was coming along with us on the way there. I also tried to make sure that everyone was properly introduced. By the time we arrived in Spain, I felt very comfortable in the group. We were met at the airport by the organisers of the holiday and driven to the countryside where we would be climbing.*

*The next day we all walked to the area in which we would be climbing. We were to climb in pairs but not with the same person all the time. In rock climbing you are attached to your partner by a rope. One person is responsible for 'belaying' the other. The belayer stays on the ground as an anchor while the other person climbs to the top of the wall. The wall is a section of the mountain. Each person has a harness and the rope is threaded through both harnesses and held in place by a belay device. A belay device is like a big clip that is attached to the rope and the harness of the belayer and this secures the person climbing up the wall. If the person climbing up the wall slips, the belayer has to secure the rope by yanking it hard down through the belay device so the climber immediately stops slipping. In order for this to work, both partners need to ensure they are properly trained. As everyone on the trip was a member of my climbing club, I was confident they had been trained properly as this is a requirement of membership. It also requires a lot of mutual trust between the climbers as your safety/life is in the hands of the person belaying you. Before you are able to climb both climbers check each other's ropes are tied in securely with the correct knot. Once the climber has reached the top they come down and alternate. We had a really good day climbing. At the end of the day we walked back down the mountain to where we were staying. After a long day of climbing, I was too tired to carry the rope myself and also felt I may slip walking back down the mountain. I asked if we could take turns carrying it. My companions were more than happy to help and we all had a turn to carry the rope.*

**Positive indicators** Yes

Understands own role in a team.

Actively supports and assists the team to reach their objectives.

Is approachable and friendly to others.

Makes time to get to know people.

Co-operates with and supports others.

Offers to help other people.

Asks for and accepts help when needed.

Develops mutual trust and confidence in others.

Willingly takes on unpopular or routine tasks.

Contributes to team objectives no matter what the direct personal benefit may be.

Acknowledges that there is often a need to be a member of more than one team.

Takes pride in their team and promotes their team's performance to others.

*General observations*

# Account 2

*The situation was that Special Constables were required to cover New Year's Eve on Public Order and Anti-Social Behaviour patrol. Many were reluctant to cover it as it was an unsocial work time and because of the nature of the duty. Realising the necessity to provide as much high visibility as possible of police presence, I volunteered.*

*I encouraged my contemporaries to also volunteer, pointing out the benefits to themselves as it would give them valuable experience and increase our standing with regulars. As a result two more volunteered.*

*At briefing we were told to perform high-visibility foot patrol throughout the night covering the centre of the town. We were deployed in pairs with a total of eight, mixed between regulars and specials to maximise use of resources and increase uniform visibility on the street and to ensure the safety of each officer. This helped to ensure public safety and reassurance. As per briefing we were to complete foot patrol and be at the clock tower at 23.30 to prevent members of the public climbing the tower and injuring themselves or others or the building. At briefing I introduced myself to all the other officers.*

*To ensure officer safety and to maximise co-operation between officers we monitored the radio at all times and gave regular updates of our locations. We were always aware of the whereabouts of other team members so could provide back up quickly. I was aware that at any time during the shift if there was a serious disorder we may be deployed elsewhere.*

*As I had considerable local knowledge of the area and my colleague had only just transferred in, I was able to contribute by suggesting likely hot-spots for public disorder and anti-social behaviour.*

*As a result, all incidents of anti-social behaviour were dealt with quickly and effectively, due partly to the larger number of officers working well together and partly due to public awareness of our presence.*

*I learnt a lot working with the team that night. They were professional at all times and I felt proud to have worked with them.*

*By volunteering on one of the busiest nights of the year I felt my presence was valued by the other officers and I was able to assist in three arrests increasing my personal knowledge and experience. One of the arrests was of a youth carrying a small quantity of drugs and as we had to take him to his home I was able to advise his parents on how he could receive help with this.*

*I felt the team effort had been enhanced by my contribution. It also established me as a respected team member and I was thanked and told that I could work with any of the officers in the future whenever I was able.*

**Positive indicators**                                                                **Yes**

Understands own role in a team.

Actively supports and assists the team to reach their objectives.

Is approachable and friendly to others.

Makes time to get to know people.

Co-operates with and supports others.

Offers to help other people.

Asks for and accepts help when needed.

Develops mutual trust and confidence in others.

Willingly takes on unpopular or routine tasks.

Contributes to team objectives no matter what the direct personal benefit may be.

Acknowledges that there is often a need to be a member of more than one team.

Takes pride in their team and promotes their team's performance to others.

*General observations*

# Account 3

*A time when I have had to co-operate with others was during high school when I took part in a group activity day. This involved approximately 150 students who were split into groups of about ten students each.*

*The aim of the activity day was to work as a team to complete a course of tasks. All tasks required each member to rely on their teammates. The objective was to test students' teamwork skills and to improve on the areas necessary.*

*Examples of some of the tasks were:*

- *A team member would be blindfolded. He or she would need to make their way around several sections where another team member would be waiting to instruct them on what needed to be done.*

- *The whole team had to get from one end of the room to another at the same time by only using two wooden boards to stand on.*

- *One half of the team were told correctly how to build a raft and then had to relay this information to the second half of the group while they built it.*

*During the activities, I found myself giving instructions and taking instructions. This was the case with all of the members of the group so that our teamworking skills could be tested from all angles. When I was in the role of giving instructions I remained calm and spoke very clearly so as not to confuse the person taking the instructions. I co-operated well with others who were also giving instructions alongside me because I had to take into consideration that others have different views and therefore may have a better way of tackling a problem than myself. When I was the person that had to complete the task I had to be very open to take suggestions. I needed to ask for and accept help when needed. It was also important for me to develop mutual trust and confidence in my team members.*

*Every time we came to another task on the course we decided how things would be done by asking members to put their hand up if they thought doing this task would be their strong point or if instructing in this task would be their strong point. If one rather than several had to be chosen, he or she was chosen in accordance to alphabetical order of first names. However, as we continued we ensured that everyone had a chance by not choosing the same person twice unless everyone had taken a turn.*

*To ensure that the team got the results that they wanted I helped to maintain a good morale. I regularly praised my teammates so that their confidence did not go down when facing a difficult task or if something went wrong. When a shy teammate was unsure about anything I would give a quick 'pep talk' to get their energy flowing.*

*By taking part in the above team activity day I saw many benefits for myself. First of all I had huge amounts of fun. I was able to work with many students that I would not have naturally chosen to work with. That was a great experience because it helped me to see how I could work well with people whom I may not have initially thought I could. The activity day taught me how to take instructions from others and that I do not always know best. Many others had fantastic ideas, which proved to me that listening was very important. I also learnt that I had to think carefully about my choice of words when giving instructions because people can often find it difficult when having to understand others' ideas.*

**Positive indicators**                                                                **Yes**

Understands own role in a team.

Actively supports and assists the team to reach their objectives.

Is approachable and friendly to others.

Makes time to get to know people.

Co-operates with and supports others.

Offers to help other people.

Asks for and accepts help when needed.

Develops mutual trust and confidence in others.

Willingly takes on unpopular or routine tasks.

Contributes to team objectives no matter what the direct personal benefit may be.

Acknowledges that there is often a need to be a member of more than one team.

Takes pride in their team and promotes their team's performance to others.

*General observations*

## Account 1 discussion

| Positive indicators | Yes |
|---|---|
| Understands own role in a team. | ✓ |
| Actively supports and assists the team to reach their objectives. | ✓ |
| Is approachable and friendly to others. | |
| Makes time to get to know people. | ✓ |
| Co-operates with and supports others. | ✓ |
| Offers to help other people. | ✓ |
| Asks for and accepts help when needed. | ✓ |
| Develops mutual trust and confidence in others. | |
| Willingly takes on unpopular or routine tasks. | ✓ |
| Contributes to team objectives no matter what the direct personal benefit may be. | ✓ |
| Acknowledges that there is often a need to be a member of more than one team. | |
| Takes pride in their team and promotes their team's performance to others. | |

### General observations

1. This account has scored very highly due to the fact that the candidate has described in detail the various influences impacting on her role in the team.
2. Other roles are also considered.
3. Perhaps the word 'I' could be used more extensively.
4. This account would benefit from the use of SARA which may enable the other competencies to be included.
5. It is unlikely that the full five minutes will be taken by this account.

## Account 2 discussion

| Positive indicators | Yes |
|---|---|
| Understands own role in a team. | ✓ |
| Actively supports and assists the team to reach their objectives. | ✓ |
| Is approachable and friendly to others. | ✓ |
| Makes time to get to know people. | ✓ |
| Co-operates with and supports others. | ✓ |
| Offers to help other people. | ✓ |
| Asks for and accepts help when needed. | |

Develops mutual trust and confidence in others.

Willingly takes on unpopular or routine tasks. ✓

Contributes to team objectives no matter what the direct personal benefit may be. ✓

Acknowledges that there is often a need to be a member of more than one team. ✓

Takes pride in their team and promotes their team's performance to others. ✓

### General observations
1. This account scored well against the competencies.

2. Although the account scores well, it does not sound contrived.

3. Excellent use of SARA.

4. Appropriate use of the word 'I' in this context.

## Account 3 discussion

**Positive indicators** **Yes**

Understands own role in a team. ✓

Actively supports and assists the team to reach their objectives. ✓

Is approachable and friendly to others. ✓

Makes time to get to know people. ✓

Co-operates with and supports others. ✓

Offers to help other people. ✓

Asks for and accepts help when needed. ✓

Develops mutual trust and confidence in others. ✓

Willingly takes on unpopular or routine tasks.

Contributes to team objectives no matter what the direct personal benefit may be. ✓

Acknowledges that there is often a need to be a member of more than one team.

Takes pride in their team and promotes their team's performance to others.

### General observations
1. The account given scores well against the objectives.

2. Some of the competencies are woven into the account but this is done appropriately, e.g. *I co-operated well with others, I needed to ask for and accept help when needed* and *important for me to develop mutual trust*.

3. Although not explicit, this account employs the use of SARA and will assist the candidate during the five-minute exposition.

# Using the language of the competencies

You may wonder if weaving the language of the competencies into your account is appropriate. For instance, the third account borrowed much of the terminology used in the indicators of the competency. However, it was used in a way that complemented the account and didn't come across as contrived. The following, on the other hand, would be inappropriate:

> *I felt I understood my role in the team and I actively supported and assisted the team to reach their objectives. I am approachable and friendly to others and I make time to get to know people. I co-operate and support people.*

This 'account' would be inappropriate because it lacks a specific context and an explanation of how the competency was achieved. General bland statements are not acceptable; you need to provide 'evidence' by giving examples. According to Malthouse and Roffey-Barentsen (2009, p5), when writing an account you should consider the following:

- The recipient – who will be receiving your communication?

- The style – is your approach to be formal or informal?

- The level of familiarity – is it appropriate to be familiar with the person?

- The beginning/end – how should you start and finish?

Although in the above the authors were referring to the written exercises, the considerations are similar for the interview process.

- Treat the recipient with respect and speak to them as you would a respected elder.

- The style of language should be formal: no slang, and certainly no mild swear words or abbreviations.

- The assessor is not a friend and so should not be spoken to as such. This is a professional relationship so you should not be familiar with the assessor.

- If you employ the mnemonic SARA your beginning will be a description of the situation and the end could be, *What I learned from this is that. . .* Ending in a definite way will enable the assessor to ask the prompt questions referred to in Chapter 1.

# Summary

This chapter has focused on the National Core Competency Team working, identifying the required level for the competency as well as the positive and negative indicators. It has discussed example accounts, identifying strengths and areas which can be improved.

Team working is a competency that candidates appear to find both relatively easy and enjoyable. You notice that one of the candidates described their experiences at school, another at work, and another during a more social type of event. All of these situations are appropriate.

As stated before, it is important to refer to yourself within the competency. Culturally, candidates do not want to appear overconfident or perhaps pushy. However, this is the time to explain what you did within a team; state your actions clearly.

Although some use of the language used in the competencies and positive indicators is acceptable, you need to make sure that you do not use general, bland statements, but substantiate your account by giving relevant examples.

# References

Malthouse, R and Roffey-Barentsen, J (2009) *Written Exercises for the Recruit Assessment Process.* Exeter: Learning Matters

# Chapter 3

## Community and customer focus

## Introduction

This chapter concentrates on the National Core Competency Community and customer focus, identifying the required level for the competency as well as the positive and negative indicators. Next, it discusses a number of accounts candidates have used during their interviews as examples. You are invited to identify which of the positive indicators are evident in the accounts and how they could be improved. Further, the chapter explains how, by employing critical thinking skills, you can adapt your accounts to address different competencies.

The competency Community and customer focus is defined below.

> *3. Community and Customer focus*
> *Focuses on the customer and provides a high-quality service that is tailored to meet their individual needs. Understands the communities that are served and shows an active commitment to policing that reflects their needs and concerns.*

The required level is as follows.

> *Required level*
> *Provides a high level of service to customers. Maintains contact with customers, works out what they need and responds to them.*

Further to the above are the positive indicators. These are a list of the behaviours that you will be expected to demonstrate during the assessment centre process (they have also been previously referred to as 'criteria'). During the assessment centre process you will be tested three times on each of the competencies. This means that you do not have to ensure that each of the positive indicators is addressed in every account. Further, although the indicators are considered during the interview, they also apply to other parts of the assessment centre process such as the interactive exercises and the written test.

## Positive indicators

- Presents an appropriate image to the public and other organisations.

- Supports strategies that aim to build an organisation that reflects the community it serves.

- Focuses on the customer in all activities.

- Tries to sort out customers' problems as quickly as possible.

- Apologises when they are at fault or have made mistakes.

- Responds quickly to customer requests.

- Makes sure that customers are satisfied with the service they receive.

- Manages customer expectations.

- Keeps customers updated on progress.

- Balances customer needs with organisational needs

## Negative indicators

A list of negative indicators identifies behaviour which is not wanted.

- Is not customer-focused and does not consider individual needs.

- Does not tell customers what is going on.

- Presents an unprofessional image to customers.

- Only sees a situation from their own view, not from the customer's view.

- Shows little interest in the customer – only deals with their immediate problem.

- Does not respond to the needs of the local community.

- Focuses on organisational issues rather than customer needs.

- Does not make the most of opportunities to talk to people in the community.

- Slow to respond to customers' requests.

- Fails to check that the customers' needs have been met.

It is good practice to read through the negative indicators as they indicate exactly what you must not do. By changing the negative indicator to a positive statement you will ensure you are doing things in the correct way. For instance, negative indicator 'does not tell customers what is going on', can be changed to 'does tell customers what is going on', which can be evidenced in your account.

# Account examples

The candidates were asked to:

*Tell me about a time when you have assisted a community or group of people.*

> **TASK 1**
>
> Consider the following three accounts and:
>
> (a) Identify which of the positive indicators are demonstrated in each account.
>
> (b) Think about how each could be improved.
>
> (c) Note any other general observations you may have.
>
> The positive indicators have been reproduced at the end of each account for your use and there is space for general observations.
>
> Suggested answers are provided at the end of the chapter. However do be aware that here you are only assessing the written word and not a person in an interview situation.

# Account 1

Two years ago, I volunteered to be part of a programme, run by the local council, to help primary school children learn about issues they may have as they prepare for secondary school. The programme had many different scenarios, such as: trusting strangers, health and safety and what to do in a fire situation.

I was part of the sports development scenario, where one other volunteer and I had to design an exercise to show children that exercise can be fun. We also taught them simple dietary requirements they should fulfil to live a healthy life, such as 'five a day'. For five days I had to interact with large groups of children and teachers. It was my task to ensure that all the children could understand and had a positive experience, as this would encourage them to take on board the information I was giving them. I made sure that I was focused on them as a group but also individually if required. For example, one child needed one-to-one help, which I gave. Each group had approximately ten people in it and the scenario only lasted eight minutes. This meant I needed to interact quickly and effectively with the whole group. This programme was adopted by every primary school in the local area, so there were a variety of needs and requirements that I needed to adapt to. On one occasion I had to remain calm and understanding when I dealt with children with learning needs such as ADHD. The children found it hard to concentrate and became distracted and troublesome. I quickly identified this problem, and adapted how I was interacting with them: instead of just talking I used a more hands-on approach. I tried to make sure that my explanations were short and the active parts of the scenario were longer, as they would enjoy these and I could teach them while they were being active. I felt that this adaptation was necessary to accompany the needs of the whole group. I also had to plan for wheelchair users, inventing a game that would teach them the benefits of keeping fit. As they could not do the same exercises as the other children, which involved skipping, I made a slalom for them and wheelchair basketball games.

I found this experience really positive and I thoroughly enjoyed working with my local community, which was benefiting children and their future. I felt that I made a difference to their lives even in the short time that I was with them.

**Positive indicators** Yes

Presents an appropriate image to the public and other organisations.

Supports strategies that aim to build an organisation that reflects the community it serves.

Focuses on the customer in all activities.

Tries to sort out customers' problems as quickly as possible.

Apologises when they are at fault or have made mistakes.

Responds quickly to customer requests.

Makes sure that customers are satisfied with the service they receive.

Manages customer expectations.

Keeps customers updated on progress.

Balances customer needs with organisational needs.

*General observations*

# Account 2

*As a Police Community Support Officer, and part of the Safer Neighbourhood Team, I was told by members of the community who use a designated park to walk their dogs, that they had been experiencing anti-social behaviour and that the park has became a hub for the drug users and dealers.*

*After listening carefully to the dog walkers' concerns, I went to the park. I noticed a lot of graffiti, broken gates and benches, the grass was high and not maintained, there was no lighting, and I also found used needles and condoms. I immediately went to the office and checked the police computer to see if there were any reports of crime in the park, and contacted the council to ask them if they had any complaints from residents.*

*After gathering relevant information from a range of sources, it was obvious the park was not safe for the community. I took personal responsibility to give the community the high customer service they deserve as I decided to launch a dog watch scheme. I discussed the idea with my team, and I asked them for their help and support. I also asked my colleagues from the dog unit for advice and guidance, and asked them to attend the lunch date for the dog watch and give the dog walkers a talk on the dog regulations. I also asked the council for their help in cleaning and maintaining the park. I kept the local community updated on progress, and maintained contact with them, and I also apologised to them that the problem was not dealt with earlier.*

*The dog watch lunch was a success and I felt proud with a job well done. I have been able to build a good relationship with dog walkers and members of the community who use the park.*

**Positive indicators**                                                          Yes

Presents an appropriate image to the public and other organisations.

Supports strategies that aim to build an organisation that reflects
the community it serves.

Focuses on the customer in all activities.

Tries to sort out customers' problems as quickly as possible.

Apologises when they are at fault or have made mistakes.

Responds quickly to customer requests.

Makes sure that customers are satisfied with the service they receive.

Manages customer expectations.

Keeps customers updated on progress.

Balances customer needs with organisational needs.

*General observations*

# Account 3

*This incident happened while I was working at an equestrian centre. In the summer holidays there was a group of traveller children that used to hang around near the stables. They had developed a bit of a bad reputation with the local residents and if there was ever any crime in the area it would be blamed on them. The children used to come to the stables and had asked the manager in the past if they could have a ride but as they had no money to pay for it, they were not allowed to. The yard manager seemed quite against having them around and often referred to them using derogatory language. I felt that this was unfair and discriminatory behaviour so I set about trying to help them. I persuaded the yard manager that it would be a good idea to get the group of children on our side and if we could get them working with us rather than against us, everyone could benefit from it. I invited the children to come to the stables for a 'Taster day', where they could come and see what work we do, meet the horses and staff and have a ride at the end of the day. If any of them wanted to become regular helpers after that day then we would allow them to come down and help out in return for lessons. Some of the other staff were against this at first so I took charge of the organisation and running of the day. I devised some fun activities for the children and after their initial shyness, they got stuck in and really enjoyed themselves. At the end of the day when they had their riding lesson, some of their parents came down to watch and thanked me for giving them a chance. They explained that although their children weren't angels they were good kids and would be happy to help out for some free lessons. After the taster day four of the children came back regularly to help out. This helped them to lose the stigma that many of the local residents had given them and because they were always at the stables, it kept them off the streets and getting into trouble.*

*At the end of the summer holidays, I organised a barbeque for the children, their friends and family. By this point the staff had forged relationships with the children and levels of mutual trust had been developed. As a result of the children being at the stables most of the time, the local residents had stopped complaining about them and some of them had even started to get to know them from being at the stables. All in all, the children, their families and the local residents all benefitted and were very grateful for my actions.*

| Positive indicators | Yes |
|---|---|
| Presents an appropriate image to the public and other organisations. | |
| Supports strategies that aim to build an organisation that reflects the community it serves. | |
| Focuses on the customer in all activities. | |
| Tries to sort out customers' problems as quickly as possible. | |
| Apologises when they are at fault or have made mistakes. | |
| Responds quickly to customer requests. | |
| Makes sure that customers are satisfied with the service they receive. | |
| Manages customer expectations. | |
| Keeps customers updated on progress. | |
| Balances customer needs with organisational needs. | |

## General observations

## Account 1 discussion

| Positive indicators | Yes |
| --- | --- |
| Presents an appropriate image to the public and other organisations. | ✓ |
| Supports strategies that aim to build an organisation that reflects the community it serves. | ✓ |
| Focuses on the customer in all activities. | ✓ |
| Tries to sort out customers' problems as quickly as possible. | ✓ |
| Apologises when they are at fault or have made mistakes. | |
| Responds quickly to customer requests. | |
| Makes sure that customers are satisfied with the service they receive. | |
| Manages customer expectations. | ✓ |
| Keeps customers updated on progress. | |
| Balances customer needs with organisational needs. | |

### *General observations*

1. In general the account is strong, benefiting from matching many of the competencies.

2. An introduction would be useful. This would enable the assessor to better understand why the candidate is there.

3. The use of SARA is recommended as this would add structure to the account.

4. This account also addresses elements of other competencies such as Problem-solving, Personal responsibility and Respect for race and diversity.

## Account 2 discussion

| Positive indicators | Yes |
| --- | --- |
| Presents an appropriate image to the public and other organisations. | ✓ |
| Supports strategies that aim to build an organisation that reflects the community it serves. | ✓ |
| Focuses on the customer in all activities. | ✓ |
| Tries to sort out customers' problems as quickly as possible. | ✓ |
| Apologises when they are at fault or have made mistakes. | |
| Responds quickly to customer requests. | |
| Makes sure that customers are satisfied with the service they receive. | ✓ |
| Manages customer expectations. | ✓ |

Keeps customers updated on progress.

Balances customer needs with organisational needs.

### General observations

1. This example represents one of the less pleasant aspects of a community officer's work. However, it is no less suitable because of this.

2. Some terminology can be described in greater detail, for example, what is a dog watch scheme exactly?

3. In general terms the account comes across as being organised and well thought through; however, it would benefit by including more detail which will enable the candidate to fill the five minutes available

4. This account may also be suitable for Problem-solving, Personal responsibility and possibly Team working.

## Account 3 discussion

| Positive indicators | Yes |
|---|---|
| Presents an appropriate image to the public and other organisations. | ✓ |
| Supports strategies that aim to build an organisation that reflects the community it serves. | ✓ |
| Focuses on the customer in all activities. | ✓ |
| Tries to sort out customers' problems as quickly as possible. | ✓ |
| Apologises when they are at fault or have made mistakes. | |
| Responds quickly to customer requests. | ✓ |
| Makes sure that customers are satisfied with the service they receive. | ✓ |
| Manages customer expectations. | ✓ |
| Keeps customers updated on progress. | |
| Balances customer needs with organisational needs. | ✓ |

### General observations

1. This is a particularly strong account, following a logical progression and telling a story.

2. The level of detail can be added to as this account may not last the whole five minutes.

3. This account can also be suitable for Respect for race and diversity, Problem-solving, Personal responsibility and Team working.

# Critical thinking

As you notice from the account discussions, accounts often address the indicators of more than one competency. Deciding how accounts can be adapted to meet other competencies involves the process of critical thinking.

According to Elder and Paul (1994) in Roffey-Barentsen and Malthouse (2009, p18), *Critical thinking is understood as the ability of thinkers to take charge of their own thinking*. Critical thinking does not mean that you are criticising your account in a negative way, instead it means that you analyse your account, looking at all elements in detail. To do this you need to adopt a reflective approach.

## Reflective approach

Once you have written your account, linking it to one of the competencies, you need to reflect on your work. This means that you need to think about the account, asking questions such as: *What did I do? Could I have done better? What else could I have done, but didn't?* (Hillier, 2005, p17). This will help you to identify the perspective, or emphasis, of the account, as it is written to address the positive indicators of a particular competency. To be able to match the account against other competencies, you need to change the perspective. In other words, the story remains the same but the perspective or emphasis changes. Next, consider what changes need to be made to address other positive indicators and can this be done. Finally, decide, with the changes in place, whether the account is suitable for the new competency.

Developing your critical thinking skills and reflective approach requires you to practise, demanding effort. However, there are rewards as they enable you to make better sense of your account and of what has taken place, which in turn assists you to make appropriate decisions.

# Summary

This chapter has focused on the National Core Competency Community and customer focus, identifying the required level for the competency as well as the positive and negative indicators.

It has discussed example accounts, identifying strengths and areas which can be improved, emphasising the importance of the use of SARA and a clear introduction.

Finally, as on occasion the story of an account for one competency can also be appropriate for other competencies, you can adapt the account by employing critical thinking skills and by being reflective in your approach.

# References

Hillier, Y (2005) *Reflective Teaching in further and Adult Education* (2nd edition). London: Continuum

Roffey Barentsen, J and Malthouse, R (2009) *Reflective Practice in the Lifelong Learning Sector.* Exeter: Learning Matters

# Chapter 4
## Effective communication

## Introduction

This chapter concentrates on the National Core Competency Effective Communication, identifying the required level for the competency as well as the positive and negative indicators. As in previous chapters, it discusses a number of accounts candidates have used during their interviews as examples. You are invited to identify which of the positive indicators are evident in the accounts and how they could be improved. Further, it gives some guidance on how to communicate effectively.

The competency Effective communication is defined below.

> *4. Effective communication*
> *Communicates ideas and information effectively, both verbally and in writing. Uses language and a style of communication that is appropriate to the situation and people being addressed. Makes sure others understand what is going on.*

The required level is indicated here.

> *Required level*
> *Communicates all needs, instructions and decisions clearly. Adapts the style of communication to meet the needs of the audience. Checks for understanding.*

Further to the above are the positive indicators, which is a list of the behaviours that you will be expected to demonstrate during the assessment centre process (they have also been referred to as the 'criteria' previously within this book). Within this core competency not all the positive indicators will apply, as you will see. Read the following and ask yourself which of these will be suitable for inclusion within the interview exercises:

## Positive indicators

- Deals with issues directly.
- Clearly communicates needs and instructions.
- Clearly communicates management decisions and policy, and the reasons behind them.
- Communicates face-to-face wherever possible and if appropriate.
- Speaks with authority and confidence.

- Changes the style of communication to meet the needs of the audience.

- Manages group discussions effectively.

- Summarises information to check people understand it.

- Supports arguments and recommendations effectively in writing.

- Produces well-structured reports and written summaries.

You will notice that some of the criteria above may not be demonstrated within the interview itself. For example, 'Produces well-structured reports and written summaries,' will be evidenced within the written test. Others may also be tested within the interactive exercises.

## Negative indicators

A list of negative indicators identifies behaviour which is not wanted, as listed below. Read through the list and ask if any can be applied (or has applied) to you.

- Is hesitant, nervous and uncertain when speaking.

- Speaks without first thinking through what to say.

- Uses inappropriate language or jargon.

- Speaks in a rambling way.

- Does not consider the target audience.

- Avoids answering difficult questions.

- Does not give full information without being questioned.

- Writes in an unstructured way.

- Uses poor spelling, punctuation and grammar.

- Assumes others understand what has been said without actually checking.

- Does not listen and interrupts at inappropriate times.

The indicator 'uses inappropriate language or jargon' needs further explanation. Inappropriate language such as swearing and the use of *derogatory words some people use to describe others* (Malthouse, Kennard and Roffey-Barentsen, 2009, p13) is unacceptable. However, the use of jargon, often used by people working for large or specialist organisations, is considered exclusionary for the listener and therefore must also be avoided.

It is good practice to read through the negative indicators as they indicate exactly what you must not do. By changing the negative indicator to a positive statement you will ensure you are doing things in the correct way. For instance, negative indicator 'speaks without first thinking through what to say', can be changed to 'speaks after thinking through what to say', which can be evidenced in your account.

# Account examples

The candidates were asked to:

*Tell me about a time when you have had to alter your method of communication to suit the needs of another.*

---

**TASK 1**

Consider the following three accounts and:

(a) Identify which of the positive indicators are demonstrated in each account.

(b) Think about how each could be improved.

(c) Note any other general observations you may have.

The positive indicators have been reproduced at the end of each account for your use and there is space for general observations.

Suggested answers are provided at the end of the chapter. However, do be aware that here you are only assessing the written word and not a person in an interview situation.

---

# Account 1

*I am currently employed in the centre of the city as a tourist officer. Working in such an iconic area attracts a considerable amount of tourists, all coming from a multitude of different countries all around the world. As I wear a uniform I am frequently approached by tourists and asked for directions to attractions, restaurants, etc., and with their limited English and my inability to speak their language I am often faced with communication problems.*

*I know that in order to communicate effectively and thus successfully, I initially have to do what is described as encoding the message correctly so the recipient can then try to decode the message I have just sent. It's a two way thing where the sender and recipient have to fulfil their part of the process for this to work because they both have to encode and decode everything.*

*As I know this because of my training, once I have been asked the question and I have understood what they are trying to ask I firstly respond as I would normally by using everyday sort of language. If the person does not understand, I know that they have not decoded what I have encoded, so I then repeat what I have said, this time slowing my speech down, giving them more time to decode what it was and then encode their answer. Failing this I change my sentence. If this still fails to work, I rephrase my sentence again, this time using simplistic terms that someone from another country just beginning to learn English might be taught. I also use non-verbal facial expressions, gestures, intonation, inflection and body language. As body language is a large portion of communication, this almost always has the desired affect. I assume this method works as they always say thank you and head in the direction I point them in.*

**Positive indicators** Yes

Deals with issues directly.

Clearly communicates needs and instructions.

Clearly communicates management decisions and policy, and the reasons behind them.

Communicates face-to-face wherever possible and if appropriate.

Speaks with authority and confidence.

Changes the style of communication to meet the needs of the audience.

Manages group discussions effectively.

Summarises information to check people understand it.

Supports arguments and recommendations effectively in writing.

Produces well-structured reports and written summaries.

*General observations*

# Account 2

*When my parents bought the guest house, I worked there on weekends and after finishing school I ran the guest house single-handed for six months. We then had to find another person to run the guest house due to the fact that I was about to go to college. It took ages to find someone suitable and the lack of manpower meant that at that time I was worked off my feet.*

*We finally found someone to work in the guest house, therefore I had to teach her how to run the guest house on her own. This is an example of when I had to change my communication skills. The lady that my father had employed was from Eastern Europe and she did not understand much English. I altered my communication by talking a lot slower and clearer due to me having a strong accent, and I expressed myself by using body language, e.g. hand gestures and different tones in my voice. I also spoke appropriately, for example I used basic English as using complicated words would not have been appropriate.*

**Positive indicators**                                                    **Yes**

Deals with issues directly.

Clearly communicates needs and instructions.

Clearly communicates management decisions and policy, and the reasons behind them.

Communicates face-to-face wherever possible and if appropriate.

Speaks with authority and confidence.

Changes the style of communication to meet the needs of the audience.

Manages group discussions effectively.

Summarises information to check people understand it.

Supports arguments and recommendations effectively in writing.

Produces well-structured reports and written summaries.

*General observations*

# Account 3

*A time when I have had to alter my method of communication to suit the needs of another was during an incident, which involved my grandmother, my auntie and myself. My grandmother, whom I had lived with since birth, was critically ill in hospital. She suffered from extreme diabetes and was facing a triple heart bypass. Due to her diabetes and age combined, the doctors informed us that there would only be approximately 40 per cent chance of survival. This was an extremely difficult piece of information to take in. My auntie, who was not present to hear this information, was unaware of what my grandmother was facing. Therefore I took it upon myself to inform her.*

*I was fully aware that my auntie would find this information very upsetting and difficult to take in. This is because my auntie would have had to come to terms with the fact that there was a large chance that her mother would not make it through the operation. Knowing that one's mother could potentially die would have huge psychological and emotional effects on anyone. Therefore, it was very important for me to alter my method of communication accordingly to account for this.*

*To deliver the message, there were many factors I had to take into account. My first decision to make was when would I tell my auntie the information. I decided that it would best to inform her as soon as possible as it was only fair that she knew about her mother's conditions as everyone else did. I then had to decide where to tell her. I chose to tell her at her own home when no one else was present. This was because I thought it would be best that she was in familiar surrounds when I told her so that she could find it easier to remain calm and secure. Also because I knew that there would be complete privacy. I wanted to ensure that no one else was present so that the situation would remain uninterrupted and calm. As I had never had to deliver this kind of message to my auntie I was unaware of how she may react so therefore I had to be prepared to expect the unexpected. How I told her was also very important. I had to be as informative as possible, while also staying very calm. I used a very soft voice and spoke slowly and clearly. When I was informing my auntie of the news about my grandmother, I began by telling her the reasons behind my grandmother's illness. I informed her that the blood flow around her heart was being blocked and that this needed to be rectified. I then went on to tell her that this could be rectified by an operation called a heart bypass and then I told her what this entailed. After I told her this, I knew I also had to tell her the percentages that the doctor told me about her survival. This is when I really had to choose my words carefully. I did not want to word it in a way which focused on her death (60 per cent chance of death) and I certainly did not want use words such as 'only' ('she only has a 40 per cent chance of survival'). So I simply said that by undergoing this operation, she has a 40 per cent chance of survival. I then went on to remind my auntie that the hospital my grandmother was in was the best heart hospital and that the doctor was fantastic. I then went on to finish by reminding my auntie the pain my grandmother was experiencing at the moment and once the operation is complete she would pain free.*

*In delivering my message there were many things I had to take into account, which resulted in me altering my method of communication to suit the needs of my auntie. I had to figure out where to tell her, when to tell her, how to tell her and what to say. If I had chosen a noisy and not so private location to tell, then it would not have kept her calm. When to tell her was important because if I had left it too late then she may have been upset at a later date knowing that she could have spent more time with her mother before the operation. How to tell her needed to be considered because if I was not calm, crying and coming across stressed then my auntie would may have thought that the situation was worse than I was letting on and therefore may have mirrored my emotions, making it harder for her to understand. What I said to her was crucial. I had to be sure not to miss any information out and also not to talk too negatively. I wanted to be honest so that she knew everything but I had to choose my words carefully so as not to be too negative. Lastly, I had to take into account the various ways that my auntie could have reacted. I had to be prepared to console her if she became extremely emotional and upset.*

*This was an extremely difficult time for myself also because my grandmother had brought me up from birth. Therefore, I had to consciously be brave and strong so that I could offer my grandmother and rest of my family as much support as possible.*

| Positive indicators | Yes |
|---|---|
| Deals with issues directly. | |
| Clearly communicates needs and instructions. | |
| Clearly communicates management decisions and policy, and the reasons behind them. | |
| Communicates face-to-face wherever possible and if appropriate. | |
| Speaks with authority and confidence. | |
| Changes the style of communication to meet the needs of the audience. | |
| Manages group discussions effectively | |
| Summarises information to check people understand it. | |
| Supports arguments and recommendations effectively in writing. | |
| Produces well-structured reports and written summaries. | |

*General observations*

## Account 1 discussion

| **Positive indicators** | **Yes** |
|---|---|
| Deals with issues directly. | ✓ |
| Clearly communicates needs and instructions. | |
| Clearly communicates management decisions and policy, and the reasons behind them. | |
| Communicates face-to-face wherever possible and if appropriate. | |
| Speaks with authority and confidence. | |
| Changes the style of communication to meet the needs of the audience. | ✓ |
| Manages group discussions effectively. | |
| Summarises information to check people understand it. | |
| Supports arguments and recommendations effectively in writing. | |
| Produces well-structured reports and written summaries. | |

### *General observations*

1. This account does not answer the question. Rather than providing an example of when the candidate has had to alter their method of communication to suit the needs of another, this account includes general observations about what they do when dealing with people who do not speak English.

2. It lacks structure.

3. It attempts to introduce a communication model but the meaning is lost with numerous references to encoding and decoding.

4. The candidate stated, *I assume this method works as they. . .*, so they have not actually checked to ensure that the person understood what was said. This is an example of a candidate exhibiting a negative indicator, 'Assumes others understand what has been said without actually checking.'

## Account 2 discussion

| Positive indicators | Yes |
|---|---|
| Deals with issues directly. | ✓ |
| Clearly communicates needs and instructions. | ✓ |
| Clearly communicates management decisions and policy, and the reasons behind them. | |
| Communicates face-to-face wherever possible and if appropriate. | |
| Speaks with authority and confidence. | |
| Changes the style of communication to meet the needs of the audience. | ✓ |
| Manages group discussions effectively. | |
| Summarises information to check people understand it. | |
| Supports arguments and recommendations effectively in writing. | |
| Produces well-structured reports and written summaries. | |

### General observations

1. This account will benefit by increasing the length of the account to fill five minutes.

2. Providing greater detail will aid clarity.

3. The allusion to 'manpower' is arguably sexist language and should be replaced with a term such as 'workforce' or 'team'.

4. The account will further benefit by the inclusion of a clearer structure.

## Account 3 discussion

| **Positive indicators** | **Yes** |
|---|---|
| Deals with issues directly. | ✓ |
| Clearly communicates needs and instructions. | ✓ |
| Clearly communicates management decisions and policy, and the reasons behind them. | |
| Communicates face-to-face wherever possible and if appropriate. | ✓ |
| Speaks with authority and confidence. | |
| Changes the style of communication to meet the needs of the audience. | ✓ |
| Manages group discussions effectively. | |
| Summarises information to check people understand it. | |
| Supports arguments and recommendations effectively in writing. | |
| Produces well-structured reports and written summaries. | |

### *General observations*

1. This is a much stronger account. It would benefit from being more structured, possibly following the SARA mnemonic.

2. A conclusion would be appropriate.

3. Analysis in relation to what they may do differently on another occasion.

4. In general this is a sound account.

During the interview process many of the criteria are judged against what you say you have done. For example, the positive indicator 'manages group discussions effectively' cannot be assessed during the assessment process. Therefore, you need to describe how you have achieved this. Other indicators, on the other hand, such as 'speaks with authority and confidence' can be assessed at the time, not relying on your account.

# Guidance on how to communicate effectively

To be able to demonstrate within the interview how well you have communicated with other people, it is important to understand some aspects of communication. One important aspect is being a good listener. The term used to describe this is 'active listening'. By employing active listening skills you demonstrate to the person who is talking that you really listen to what they have to say. The techniques that are used are:

- paraphrasing;
- reflecting / mirroring;
- emotional labelling;
- minimal encouragers.

## Paraphrasing

Paraphrasing is a summary of what has been said and demonstrates to another person that you are giving them your full attention. Further benefits of paraphrasing are that it creates empathy and rapport because it informs the other person that they have been understood.

Paraphrasing often begins with the words:

*So you are saying that . . .*

*I see, so you mean that . . .*

*Let me just get this right, you say . . .*

It further benefits communication by clarifying the definition of the content of the communication and highlights any issues that may be present. What you are doing is telling the other person what you understood from what they have said. If you find yourself communicating to a person who is flustered or becoming angry, you will find that paraphrasing will not put the person on the defensive because the words you are using are their own: they will hear that you are listening to them.

## Mirroring

Mirroring is repeating the last word or part of a phrase the person said and putting a question mark after it. For example: *Money? Drain? Tuesday?* As with paraphrasing, this method provides very precise responses because you are using the other person's words. Reflecting/mirroring asks for more information but has the advantage of not influencing the other person's thoughts. If you are involved in gathering evidence or especially when dealing with vulnerable adults or children, this can be a very useful communication tool. It is also a useful means of eliciting information when there is not enough information to ask another question. Further to verbal mirroring, consider your use of body language. When a rapport is building between the person talking and you, you find that your body language is mirroring theirs. This happens quite naturally, without thinking. For instance, if they hold their head to one side, so will you. To encourage rapport you can deliberately mirror their body language, by copying how they are sitting, holding their head, etc.

## Emotional labelling

Emotional labelling consists of listening not only to the facts but to the emotional reactions to those facts; in other words, it concentrates on the emotion behind the words and facts. For example you can observe the following:

- *You seem hurt*
- *I hear frustration*
- *You sound angry*

You do not tell a person how they are feeling but you highlight how it seems or sounds like they are feeling. Emotional labelling demonstrates that you are listening and are aware of what the person is experiencing emotionally. This may open doors to further questions that you didn't know existed.

## Minimal encouragers

Minimal encouragers is a simple technique. They are the sounds you make, especially on the telephone, to let one person know that you are there and are listening to them. Generally they are one short question or noise such as:

- *Oh*
- *U huh*
- *Really*
- *Yes*
- *Go on*

An important element of these is that they are questions, comments or sounds that are unlikely to interfere with the flow of the communication. The purpose is aimed at letting the other person know that you are listening. Body language can also be used as a minimal encourager. You can lean forward to show your interest, perhaps nod your head, or look expectantly, etc. Minimal encouragers are useful because they help build rapport and encourage the person to continue talking.

In preparation for your interview, as you are searching for suitable examples, try to introduce any of the above techniques into your communication style. Communication with others will be enhanced as a result.

# Summary

This chapter has focused on the National Core Competency Effective communication, identifying the required level for the competency as well as the positive and negative indicators.

It has discussed example accounts, identifying strengths and areas which can be improved, emphasising the importance of answering the actual question and the use of appropriate language. Finally, a number of techniques have been discussed to enhance your active listening skills, which form a part of effective communication.

# References

Cox, P (2007) *Passing the Police Recruit Assessment Process*. Exeter: Learning Matters

Malthouse, R, Kennard, P and Roffey-Barentsen, J (2009) *Interactive Exercises for the Police Recruit Assessment Process. Succeeding at Role Plays*. Exeter: Learning Matters

# Chapter 5
## Problem solving

## Introduction

This chapter concentrates on the National Core Competency Problem-solving, identifying the required level for the competency as well as the positive and negative indicators. As in previous chapters, it discusses a number of accounts candidates have used during their interviews as examples. You are invited to identify which of the positive indicators are evident in the accounts and how they could be improved. Further, it explains a model for problem-solving.

The competency Problem-solving is defined below.

> *5. Problem-solving*
> *Gathers information from a range of sources. Analyses information to identify problems and issues and makes effective decisions.*

The required level is as follows.

> *Required level*
> *Gathers enough relevant information to understand specific issues and events. Uses information to identify problems and draw conclusions. Makes good decisions.*

Further to the above are the positive indicators. These are a list of the behaviours that you will be expected to demonstrate during the assessment centre process (they have also been previously referred to as 'criteria'). During the assessment centre process you will be tested three times on each of the competencies. This means that you do not have to ensure that each of the positive indicators is addressed in every account. Further, although the indicators are considered during the interview, they also apply to other parts of the assessment centre process such as the interactive exercises and the written test.

### Positive indicators

- Identifies where to get information and gets it.
- Gets as much information as is appropriate on all aspects of a problem.
- Separates relevant information from irrelevant information and important information from unimportant information.

- Takes in information quickly and accurately.

- Reviews all the information gathered to understand the situation and to draw logical conclusions.

- Identifies and links causes and effects.

- Identifies what can and cannot be changed.

- Takes a systematic approach to solving problems.

- Remains impartial and avoids jumping to conclusions.

- Refers to procedures and precedents, as necessary, before making decisions.

- Makes good decisions that take account of all relevant factors.

## Negative indicators

A list of negative indicators identifies behaviour which is not wanted, as listed below.

- Doesn't deal with problems in detail and does not identify underlying issues.

- Does not gather enough information before coming to conclusions.

- Does not consult other people who may have extra information.

- Does not research background.

- Shows no interest in gathering or using intelligence.

- Does not gather evidence.

- Makes assumptions about facts of a situation.

- Does not recognise problems until they have become significant issues.

- Gets stuck in the detail of complex situations and cannot see the main issues.

- Reacts without considering all the angles.

- Becomes distracted by minor issues.

It is good practice to read through the negative indicators as they indicate exactly what you must not do. By changing the negative indicator to a positive statement you will ensure you are doing things in the correct way. For instance, negative indicator 'makes assumptions about facts of a situation' can be changed to 'does not makes assumptions about facts of a situation', which can be evidenced in your account.

# Account examples

The candidates were asked to:

*Tell me about a specific time when you had to gather information to solve a problem.*

---

**TASK 1**

Consider the following three accounts and:

(a) Identify which of the positive indicators are demonstrated in each account.

(b) Think about how each could be improved.

(c) Note any other general observations you may have.

The positive indicators have been reproduced at the end of each account for your use and there is space for general observations.

Suggested answers are provided at the end of the chapter. However, do be aware that here you are only assessing the written word and not a person in an interview situation.

---

# Account 1

*Universities work in partnership with the NHS to train future nurses. Funding for their training is provided by the NHS. Student nurses spend half of their time at the university and the other half out on clinical placements. Part of student nurse training involves attendance at mandatory sessions very early on in their training, both theory and practice. Each cohort had approximately 350 students. Half of the cohort would be out on clinical placement and the other half attending at the university.*

*The problem was getting all nursing students to attend mandatory 'Moving and handling people' training before being allowed out on clinical placement. This had to occur within the first two weeks of their course. It was a problem because the university had a legal requirement to deliver this training. It was a problem because it was in the contract with the NHS that the university must deliver this training. It was my problem because I was the 'Moving and handling people' lead person, so it was my responsibility to get it done. It was a problem because there were only three skills laboratories available for this session, one of which was not adequately equipped. Another problem was the student:trainer ratio. Current acceptable professional standards dictate a 7:1 ratio. Another major problem was that despite being told how imperative it was to attend and the implications of non-attendance, many students approached the subject in a very casual manner, choosing not to attend. So, apart from going to their homes and dragging them kicking and screaming to the sessions, I had a massive problem to solve.*

*In the first instance the information I had to gather was: how many students were there? How many time slots were available in the skills laboratory? How many trainers were available to deliver the training? Was the necessary equipment available in the laboratory to deliver the training?*

*The problem got even deeper. It was not merely a case of non-attendance meaning not being allowed to go out on clinical placement. There were repercussions to this. No 'Moving and handling' training meant no clinical placement, which meant the student would have to be back-setted (withdrawn from current cohort and invited to attend at the next cohort). However, the university would have its funding withdrawn by the NHS – a major catastrophe for the university as the money would have already been allocated. So, as you can see, I had to get these students to attend 'by any means necessary'!*

*The first few times I tried to problem-solve this was by putting on extra sessions for those students who missed their sessions. As each session lasted three hours, I found myself working late into the evening and doing the same session three, four, five times over. I found I was doing a week's extra work just because the students couldn't be bothered to turn up. Word got around that I would put on another session, so they just didn't bother to attend. I realised putting on extra sessions was not the answer as I was the one receiving the 'punishment'. I was wearing myself out because of their lack of responsibility. This was not working, so I put my thinking cap on and come up with a better idea.*

*I decided to write a 'Moving and handling people' protocol. It was a contract signed by the student nurse and it laid out all the expectations of the student nurse with regard to this subject. Ultimately, it stated that they knew and fully understood the implications of non-attendance. They would be withdrawn from the course and brought before the Student Conduct Board. They would then have to give a reason (medical or death of family member), together with certificates as proof for their non-attendance. I brought this to the Clinical Skills Group for their approval and it was received positively.*

*On implementation, it was like a magic wand. Almost every student turned up for their session, and those who were absent were absent for medical reasons. I only had to do one extra session to make up for absentees. I realised that before the protocol, I was shouldering the problem myself, whereas when I turned over responsibility to the student, it had a massive turnaround. It taught them to take ownership of their actions and be prepared to pay the consequences.*

---

**Positive indicators**                                                    **Yes**

Identifies where to get information and gets it.

Gets as much information as is appropriate on all aspects of a problem.

Separates relevant information from irrelevant information and important information from unimportant information.

Takes in information quickly and accurately.

Reviews all the information gathered to understand the situation and to draw logical conclusions.

Identifies and links causes and effects.

Identifies what can and cannot be changed.

Takes a systematic approach to solving problems.

Remains impartial and avoids jumping to conclusions.

Refers to procedures and precedents, as necessary, before making decisions.

Makes good decisions that take account of all relevant factors.

---

*General observations*

# Account 2

*In my role as a communication engineer I was asked if I would be able to dismantle a door-locking system from one door and reinstall it on another in a different building. I had never done this before; however, it was very similar in principle to the communication systems we install so I said yes.*

*The door-locking system consists of two magnets, one on the top of the door and one opposite it, located in the top of the door frame; a card reader that is on the wall outside of the room, next to the door, and reads the cards members of staff have that act like a key to a lock. When the reader is swiped with the correct card it sends a signal to the two magnets that are holding the door together; they demagnetise and the door lock releases, allowing you to open it. On the inside of the room is a door release button that is used to open the door from the inside: the button is pushed and again the signal is sent to the magnets and the door is released. Once someone has opened the door from the inside or the outside, and once it is shut again the two magnets rearm, locking the door again. Inside the room is also an emergency door release panel which is a break-glass system: you break the glass and it permanently releases the magnets, leaving the door constantly open in case of fire or any other reason the room may have to be evacuated. Then there is a control panel that is situated in the room and this is responsible for receiving the signals from the release mechanisms and sending the release signals to the magnets. The control panel is connected to a main distribution box located in another building. The main distribution box collects all the information from all the different control panels located at all the locked doors across the site and then relays the information to a computer, telling the operator which doors are open, which are closed and how many times they have been opened and closed.*

*I started to dismantle the locking system from the door, making sure that I labelled all the parts and wires with what they were for, where they came from and where they went to. Once I had removed all the parts I installed a new cable from the main distribution box to the new location. The locking system was then installed around the new door and all the cables reconnected to the positions they came from.*

*I switched the system on and the magnets did not arm as they should, therefore the door was not locked. However, the release mechanisms appeared to be working.*

*I suspected the problem was related to the magnets so I checked the wires between the magnets and the control panel to see if they were in the right place and connected properly: they were.*

I contacted the computer operator to see if they could see if they were receiving information from the panel in question and whether it was reading the door as open or shut. The operator told me that they were receiving information from the panel and that the door was being read as open. From this I knew the control panel was working as it was sending and receiving signals.

Next I checked the wires between the magnets and the control panel using a continuity tester. This works by placing a probe at each end of the cable and then sending a small electrical current down one probe and taking a reading off the other probe to make sure the current passes all the way through the wire. If the current passes all the way through the wire to the other probe this means the wire is not broken anywhere. The wire was not broken. I then checked all the other wires attached to the control panel and the other components of the system to see if any of them were broken. They were not.

I wondered if I had made a mistake when I labelled the wires and parts when I originally dismantled the locking system resulting in me wiring the system up wrong, so I went to look at one of the other doors with the same locking system on. I opened the control panel and noted down where all the wires were terminated to and then went back to the panel I was working on to check if they were the same. They were.

I was stuck, I could see no reason why the magnets would not arm and lock the door. I decided to take myself away from the situation for five minutes and see if I could clear my mind and come back with fresh eyes. I went for a cup of tea. As I was drinking my tea I started to wonder if the problem had something to do with the magnets themselves as opposed to the wires and the control panel. I thought maybe one or both had been damaged somehow.

I went back to the door, opened it and looked up at the magnets. There did not seem to be any obvious damage, but as I shut the door again I noticed that the door was not actually meeting the door frame, and I wondered if the magnets had to actually touch to arm; maybe if they were not close enough to each other they were not strong enough to pull each other together. I adjusted the magnet attached to the door so that it protruded a few millimetres away from the door so that when the door shut the two magnets would touch. I shut the door and as the magnets touched I heard a clunk. I knew from the sound that the magnets had armed and that the door was locked, I pulled on the door and it would not open: the system was now working. I checked that all the door-release mechanisms were working as they should; they were, so I packed up and went on to the next job.

Afterwards, looking back on the problem it seemed so obvious what the issue was. I was a little bit annoyed with myself that I had not thought of it earlier, however I was happy that the problem was now solved and the right result was eventually achieved.

| **Positive indicators** | **Yes** |
|---|---|
| Identifies where to get information and gets it. | |
| Gets as much information as is appropriate on all aspects of a problem. | |
| Separates relevant information from irrelevant information and important information from unimportant information. | |
| Takes in information quickly and accurately. | |
| Reviews all the information gathered to understand the situation and to draw logical conclusions. | |
| Identifies and links causes and effects. | |
| Identifies what can and cannot be changed. | |
| Takes a systematic approach to solving problems. | |
| Remains impartial and avoids jumping to conclusions. | |
| Refers to procedures and precedents, as necessary, before making decisions. | |
| Makes good decisions that take account of all relevant factors. | |

*General observations*

# Account 3

*This incident occurred in my workplace, a college of further education. I work in the construction department and regularly am in charge of groups of 20 students upward. As it is not always a classroom-based subject the students naturally move around and it is impossible to know exactly where each student is all of the time.*

*It was drawn to my attention quite early on in the term that someone was stealing money and valuables from the students' lockers. This storage facility is used for the storage of the students' safety hats, gloves, boots and anything else they may require. Valuables are not supposed to be left in here as they cannot be locked. Students are advised to leave any valuables in the main lockers elsewhere on the campus as this facility is much more secure.*

*Some students, however, continued to leave their valuables in these lockers and inevitably possessions were getting stolen. Although the students were warned on many occasions not to leave their money in an unsecured place they continued to do so and more and more money was being taken.*

*The first thing I did when I was made aware of the problem was to put up signs warning the students not to leave their valuables open to thieves and to keep their eyes peeled for any suspicious activity. I spoke to all the groups and tried to convey just how wrong it is to steal something that does not belong to you. Unfortunately this had little effect and money still continued to go missing. I organised for a CCTV camera to be installed in the area but due to funding this would not be able to be installed for some time.*

*From the way I was looking at it I had two problems to solve. The first was why the students continued to leave their belongings in the unsecured lockers and the second was who was stealing the money and why. I started by meeting the students in groups and asking them why they were not using the secured lockers. It was difficult initially to derive an answer from this question because the students were reluctant to talk. They did not want to lose face or appear to be a 'grass' in front of their peers. I eventually found out from the students and also from the allocated locker plan that some of the older groups of students had taken two or more lockers, meaning that there were not enough to go round and therefore some of the newer students had to use the unsecured ones. Once I had this information it was easy to rectify. I spoke to the older students and told them they were only allowed one locker each as there were not enough to go round.*

*Once this problem was rectified I concentrated on the more pressing problem of who was stealing and why. I again asked groups of students if anyone knew anything but it seemed that no one did, or if they did they were not admitting to it. I also spoke to all staff and asked if they had noticed anyone acting suspiciously or anyone that suddenly seemed to have more money than usual. One student's name was suggested but I did not jump to conclusions at this point.*

*Eventually the CCTV was installed. By this time the thieving had lessened but it was still going on intermittently despite everyone's vigilance. I checked the CCTV regularly and I eventually caught the culprit, one of the students, in the act. I immediately summoned the student to the office and explained I had evidence of the theft. At first the student denied it but later on admitted, claiming that there was no money to come to college or for lunch and the only way to could get it was by stealing. The student felt awful but did not know what to do. Stealing is wrong, whatever the reason, so the student was punished for this according to college policy. I did, however, try to do my best to help. I spoke to the parents and the local authority about grants and funding. The parents had no idea about the problem and agreed to give some help. They also managed to obtain a grant to help even further.*

*This situation has taught me that sometimes you have to look beneath the problem if you want to fix it and that prevention is better than cure.*

---

**Positive indicators**                                                    **Yes**

Identifies where to get information and gets it.

Gets as much information as is appropriate on all aspects of a problem.

Separates relevant information from irrelevant information and important information from unimportant information.

Takes in information quickly and accurately.

Reviews all the information gathered to understand the situation and to draw logical conclusions.

Identifies and links causes and effects.

Identifies what can and cannot be changed.

Takes a systematic approach to solving problems.

Remains impartial and avoids jumping to conclusions.

Refers to procedures and precedents, as necessary, before making decisions.

Makes good decisions that take account of all relevant factors.

*General observations*

## Account 1 discussion

| **Positive indicators** | **Yes** |
| --- | --- |
| Identifies where to get information and gets it. | ✓ |
| Gets as much information as is appropriate on all aspects of a problem. | ✓ |
| Separates relevant information from irrelevant information and important information from unimportant information. | |
| Takes in information quickly and accurately. | |
| Reviews all the information gathered to understand the situation and to draw logical conclusions. | ✓ |
| Identifies and links causes and effects. | ✓ |
| Identifies what can and cannot be changed. | ✓ |
| Takes a systematic approach to solving problems. | ✓ |
| Remains impartial and avoids jumping to conclusions. | ✓ |
| Refers to procedures and precedents, as necessary, before making decisions. | ✓ |
| Makes good decisions that take account of all relevant factors. | ✓ |

### General observations

1. In general this is a very competent account in comparison to the core competencies.

2. It benefits from a clear explanation of the problem, which is contextualised, enabling the listener to understand the issues.

3. The problem is clearly defined

4. The problem-solving process is identified.

5. The resolution is described in terms that are easily understood.

## Account 2 discussion

| **Positive indicators** | **Yes** |
| --- | --- |
| Identifies where to get information and gets it. | ✓ |
| Gets as much information as is appropriate on all aspects of a problem. | ✓ |
| Separates relevant information from irrelevant information and important information from unimportant information. | |
| Takes in information quickly and accurately. | |
| Reviews all the information gathered to understand the situation and to draw logical conclusions. | ✓ |

Identifies and links causes and effects. ✓

Identifies what can and cannot be changed.

Takes a systematic approach to solving problems. ✓

Remains impartial and avoids jumping to conclusions.

Refers to procedures and precedents, as necessary, before making decisions.

Makes good decisions that take account of all relevant factors.

### General observations

1.  This is a great description of a problem and the subsequent resolution, but as the candidate describes a mechanical problem, the criteria are not met.

2.  The core competencies are designed to deal with interactions with people. Although the computer operator was referred to, most of this account details an interaction with an inanimate object.

3.  In this case it is unlikely that reworking the material would improve the account; therefore, the candidate is advised to think of a more appropriate account to meet this competency.

4.  The candidate's tenacity and attention should be applauded; this approach to a person-based problem would score well.

## Account 3 discussion

| Positive indicators | Yes |
| --- | --- |
| Identifies where to get information and gets it. | ✓ |
| Gets as much information as is appropriate on all aspects of a problem. | ✓ |
| Separates relevant information from irrelevant information and important information from unimportant information. | ✓ |
| Takes in information quickly and accurately. | ✓ |
| Reviews all the information gathered to understand the situation and to draw logical conclusions. | ✓ |
| Identifies and links causes and effects. | ✓ |
| Identifies what can and cannot be changed. | ✓ |
| Takes a systematic approach to solving problems. | ✓ |
| Remains impartial and avoids jumping to conclusions. | ✓ |
| Refers to procedures and precedents, as necessary, before making decisions. | ✓ |
| Makes good decisions that take account of all relevant factors. | ✓ |

*General observations*

1. The strength of this account lies in the fact that it explains the situation in such a way that the listener is able to comprehend what was occurring, for example it follows a logical progression by telling a story.

2. SARA employed very well.

3. There is little room for improvement within this account.

# Model for problem solving

Before a problem can be solved, you first need to identify what that problem is. The causes for the problem need to be analysed and a possible solution selected. Consider adopting a psycholateral approach, which provides an informed method of thinking, enabling you to consider the problem from a variety of perspectives before deciding on a course of action (Roffey-Barentsen and Malthouse, 2009, p42). Next, you need to find out if the solution worked: has the problem been solved? Roffey-Barentsen and Malthouse (2009) suggest CADSIE, a six-step model for problem-solving:

1. clarifying and describing the problem (Clarification);

2. analysing the plausible causes (Analysis);

3. considering alternatives (Deliberation);

4. choosing one (Selection);

5. putting it into practice (Initiation);

6. evaluating whether the problem was solved or not (Evaluation).

(Roffey-Barentsen and Malthouse, 2009, p18)

The mnemonic CADSIE, taken from the words Classification, Analysis, Deliberation, Selection, Initiation and Evaluation, enables you to approach a problem in an organised and methodical way. If you have already dealt with a problem, and you wish to record it for the interview process, using the CADSIE model enables you to consider each stage in sequence; this will assist the listener to make more sense of your account.

# Summary

This chapter has focused on the National Core Competency Problem solving, identifying the required level for the competency as well as the positive and negative indicators.

It has discussed example accounts, identifying strengths and areas which can be improved. The examples used within this competency highlight the need to think about problem-solving in terms of people. Much information can be provided by people and often the cause of the problem is people. Finally, it has explained CADSIE, a model for solving problems in an organised and methodical way.

# References

Roffey-Barentsen, J and Malthouse, R (2009) *Reflective Practice in the Lifelong Learning Sector.* Exeter: Learning Matters

# Further reading

Bacal, R (2005) *Perfect Phrases for Customer Service: Hundreds of Tools, Techniques, and Scripts for Handling any Situation*. New York: McGraw-Hill Professional

Back, K and Back, K (2005) *Assertiveness at Work: A Practical Guide to Handling Awkward Situations* (3rd Edition). New York: McGraw-Hill Professional

# Chapter 6
# Personal responsibility

## Introduction

This chapter concentrates on the National Core Competency Personal responsibility, identifying the required level for the competency as well as the positive and negative indicators. As in previous chapters, it discusses a number of accounts candidates have used during their interviews as examples. You are invited to identify which of the positive indicators are evident in the accounts and how they could be improved. Further, it explains in detail what is meant by personal responsibility in relation to customer service.

The competency Personal responsibility is defined below.

*6. Personal responsibility*
*Takes personal responsibility for making things happen and achieving results. Displays motivation commitment, perseverance and conscientiousness. Acts with a high degree of integrity.*

The required level is as follows.

*Required level*
*Takes personal responsibility for own actions and for sorting out issues or problems that arise. Is focused on achieving results to required standards and developing skills and knowledge.*

Further to the above are the positive indicators. These are a list of the behaviours that you will be expected to demonstrate during the assessment centre process (they have also been referred to previously as 'criteria'). During the assessment centre process you will be tested three times on each of the competencies. This means that you do not have to ensure that each of the positive indicators is addressed in every account. Further, although the indicators are considered during the interview, they also apply to other parts of the assessment centre process such as the interactive exercises and the written test.

## Positive indicators

- Accepts personal responsibility for own decisions and actions.

- Takes action to resolve problems and fulfil own responsibilities.

- Keeps promises and does not let colleagues down.

- Takes pride in work.

- Is conscientious in completing work on time.

- Follows things through to satisfactory conclusion.

- Displays initiative, taking on tasks without having to be asked.

- Self-motivated, showing enthusiasm and dedication to their role.

- Focuses on task even if it is routine.

- Improves own professional knowledge and keeps it up to date.

- Is open, honest and genuine, standing up for what is right.

- Makes decisions based upon ethical consideration and organisational integrity.

## Negative indicators

A list of negative indicators identifies behaviour which is not wanted, as listed below.

- Passes responsibility upwards inappropriately.

- Is not concerned about letting others down.

- Will not deal with issues, just hopes they will go away.

- Blames others rather than admitting to mistakes or looking for help.

- Unwilling to take on responsibility.

- Puts in the minimum effort that is needed to get by.

- Shows a negative and disruptive attitude.

- Shows little energy and enthusiasm for work.

- Expresses a cynical attitude to the organisation and their job.

- Gives up easily when faced with problems.

- Fails to recognise personal weaknesses and development needs.

- Makes little or no attempt to develop self or keep up to date.

It is good practice to read through the negative indicators as they indicate exactly what you must not do. By changing the negative indicator to a positive statement you will ensure you are doing things in the correct way. For instance, negative indicator 'unwilling to take on responsibility', can be changed to 'takes on responsibility', which can be evidenced in your account.

# Account examples

The candidates were asked to:

*Tell me about a time when you have volunteered for a task.*

---

**TASK 1**

Consider the following three accounts and:

(a) Identify which of the positive indicators are demonstrated in each account.

(b) Think about how each could be improved.

(c) Note any other general observations you may have.

The positive indicators have been reproduced at the end of each account for your use and there is space for general observations.

Suggested answers are provided at the end of the chapter. However do be aware that here you are only assessing the written word and not a person in an interview situation.

---

# Account 1

*Our local community is organising a Chinese language and cultural school for kids, to take place every Saturday in the community centre.*

*I was told that the centre would be an ideal place for young Chinese to be able to learn to read and write Chinese, and also for them to be able to meet other Chinese children. I thought it was an excellent idea as I attended one myself when I was younger and felt that I benefited from it in regards to learning more about my parents' culture and also learning the basics of reading and writing in Chinese.*

*I am a keen chef of oriental food, so I thought it would be an ideal opportunity for me to be able to share what I know of Chinese food and cookery with any of the students at the centre. With this I was hoping to broaden their minds and experiences.*

*It was decided that we would dedicate two hours of the Saturday to me running a cookery class at the Chinese school. The difficult task ahead was that as it was July, I would only have just over a month to organise a type of learning curriculum for these kids. Obtaining the necessary materials, ingredients and hardware would also be a challenge.*

*I identified that I would need a number of sets of cooking utensils, a stove, etc. I had some at home that I wasn't using and my family also gave me some things. I donated these temporarily to the centre.*

*The other challenge was to develop a structured and organised type of curriculum for me to be able to spend the two hours I would have with the pupils in the most constructive and efficient way possible. This I found difficult, as I knew it would take me a while to organise this from scratch by myself. So with this in mind, I then made enquiries at various establishments that offered similar foundation courses with young people in mind, and then as a result was able to construct one myself from the information I had gathered.*

*As a result, from feedback I received from the students, the course was a success and to this day I am still in contact with a number of the students who are cooking Chinese meals now at their homes.*

| Positive indicators | Yes |
|---|---|
| Accepts personal responsibility for own decisions and actions. | |
| Takes action to resolve problems and fulfil own responsibilities. | |
| Keeps promises and does not let colleagues down. | |
| Takes pride in work. | |
| Is conscientious in completing work on time. | |
| Follows things through to satisfactory conclusion. | |
| Displays initiative, taking on tasks without having to be asked. | |
| Self-motivated, showing enthusiasm and dedication to their role. | |
| Focuses on task even if it is routine. | |
| Improves own professional knowledge and keeps it up to date. | |
| Is open, honest and genuine, standing up for what is right. | |
| Makes decisions based upon ethical consideration and organisational integrity. | |

## *General observations*

*Account 2*

*A time when I volunteered for a task was when I worked for a duty-free company at an airport. It involved a colleague, a customer and myself.*

*While on my shift, I overheard a colleague trying to assist a customer but it seemed like he was having some difficulty. For a short time I observed the situation to have a better understanding of the problem. From this, I realised that the difficulty in communication was due to the language barrier. I could hear that the customer was speaking Punjabi, which is a language that I am very fluent in speaking. I knew that if I changed from my usual method of communication to instead speak Punjabi to the customer, I would be able to assist both my colleague, as he would then be able to serve the customer better, and the customer, who would be able to get the assistance she required in order to make her purchase.*

*I calmly approached my colleague and the customer and offered my assistance. I told my colleague that I overheard he was having communication problems with the customer and that I was able to speak the same language as the customer. My colleague was very appreciative of the help and accepted instantly. I then introduced myself to the customer and informed her that I was here to translate between her and my colleague. I then went on to relay the information between both parties.*

*Before offering my assistance I had to be sure that it was required. I did not want to simply rush into the situation and create a disturbance in the relationship between the customer and my colleague unless help was required. In order to be sure of this I had to remember to first ask if my assistance was required as I would not have wanted to step on my colleague's toes. Once this was done, it was also important for me to introduce myself properly to the customer, so as not to create unnecessary confusion. Another important factor that I had to take into consideration was to ensure that I did not take over the situation. I had to remember that this was still my colleague's 'sale' and he still had ownership of it.*

*By changing my method of communication to suit the needs of the people in the above situation and by taking personal responsibility to assist my colleague and the customer, I was able to help in many ways. The situation was able to be completed in a hugely shorter amount of time than it would have if I had not offered my assistance. In a worst-case scenario, the customer may simply have given up trying to communicate and left the store (a) without the product required and (b) upset/angry at the store, leaving her with negative feelings toward our duty-free outlet. Changing my method of communication to assist also meant that both the customer and my colleague could feel a sense of calm and relief and my colleague could also feel supported by his fellow worker.*

| Positive indicators | Yes |
|---|---|
| Accepts personal responsibility for own decisions and actions. | |
| Takes action to resolve problems and fulfil own responsibilities. | |
| Keeps promises and does not let colleagues down. | |
| Takes pride in work. | |
| Is conscientious in completing work on time. | |
| Follows things through to satisfactory conclusion. | |
| Displays initiative, taking on tasks without having to be asked. | |
| Self-motivated, showing enthusiasm and dedication to their role. | |
| Focuses on task even if it is routine. | |
| Improves own professional knowledge and keeps it up to date. | |
| Is open, honest and genuine, standing up for what is right. | |
| Makes decisions based upon ethical consideration and organisational integrity. | |

## General observations

# Account 3

*I work as a youth club organiser in a team of five. We work with young people aged from 9 years to 14 years who are at risk of exclusion from school or at risk of offending. These youngsters are referred to us either from schools, the Youth Offending Team or social workers.*

*We take a group and run the youth club once a week for approximately ten weeks. Prior to the start of each programme we meet to discuss the youngsters who will be attending, what we feel their needs are and how we can best meet these needs. We plan activities, outings and exercises, all of which are designed to increase their social awareness, their self-esteem and anger management.*

*At the first session that the youngsters attend we all go into the quiet room and introduce ourselves. We then ask them how they would like to see the club run and what rules they feel should be implemented. We keep a list of rules in a prominent place and add to these if they feel it's needed. We make it clear that if these rules are broken it will spoil the evening for all – we give one warning then it's suspension from the group. The young people are shown by example from the team how much better their time can be when they treat others with respect, show honesty and integrity and are kind. In the two years that the club has been running we have had never had to suspend a youth. Throughout each session we talk quietly to each youngster about how their time with us is going, whether they feel we can make improvements or do anything to improve their time with us. As we are constantly interacting with the group we are able to pick up on any problems that occur and deal with them immediately, showing respect for each individual and keeping confidentiality at all times. At the end of each session we have a team meeting when we all share information about each youth, how they are interacting with others, whether there is anything that is of concern regarding their behaviour or if they have said anything to cause concern. We are then able to highlight any areas that we need to focus on.*

*We have changed activities in the club to cater for the needs of the youngsters. We always have a quiet room doing art activities, a games room and a room to play pool and table football in. Each room is monitored and we interact with them. We also use a kitchen for refreshments and to make biscuits and cakes. Soon after the club first started I noticed that one of the young people was constantly asking for biscuits and fruit. When asked, we were told that the young person had not eaten since lunch. As it was 1900 hours, hunger had struck. After discussing this with the team I suggested we talk to the parents about whether they could provide something to eat before attending the club. Unfortunately this was not possible so I decided to teach basic cooking at each session, thus providing the youngsters with a meal if they would like it after seeking permission from the parents and carers. This gave them a social experience of sitting at a table with others, pride in their cooking skills and a good meal.*

*We involve the young people in fund-raising in the community. They plan games and events which will bring in funds for the group and it also gives them chance to interact in a positive way with the community. When they finish their time with us we organise an outing to reward them for their achievements – for instance, an evening bowling. At the end of this we present them with medals highlighting something they have been especially good at, therefore ending on a very positive note and sending them off feeling extremely proud of themselves.*

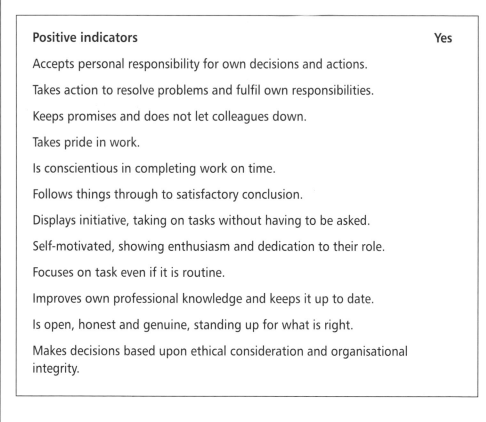

### Positive indicators                                    Yes

Accepts personal responsibility for own decisions and actions.

Takes action to resolve problems and fulfil own responsibilities.

Keeps promises and does not let colleagues down.

Takes pride in work.

Is conscientious in completing work on time.

Follows things through to satisfactory conclusion.

Displays initiative, taking on tasks without having to be asked.

Self-motivated, showing enthusiasm and dedication to their role.

Focuses on task even if it is routine.

Improves own professional knowledge and keeps it up to date.

Is open, honest and genuine, standing up for what is right.

Makes decisions based upon ethical consideration and organisational integrity.

*General observations*

## Account 1 discussion

| Positive indicators | Yes |
|---|:---:|
| Accepts personal responsibility for own decisions and actions. | ✓ |
| Takes action to resolve problems and fulfil own responsibilities. | ✓ |
| Keeps promises and does not let colleagues down. | ✓ |
| Takes pride in work. | |
| Is conscientious in completing work on time. | ✓ |
| Follows things through to satisfactory conclusion. | ✓ |
| Displays initiative, taking on tasks without having to be asked. | ✓ |
| Self-motivated, showing enthusiasm and dedication to their role. | ✓ |
| Focuses on task even if it is routine. | |
| Improves own professional knowledge and keeps it up to date. | |
| Is open, honest and genuine, standing up for what is right. | |
| Makes decisions based upon ethical consideration and organisational integrity. | |

### General observations

1. This account meets many of the positive indicators.
2. The account is positive and enthusiastic, which has the effect of the listener taking an interest.
3. It will benefit from further description and explanations to fill the five minutes.

## Account 2 discussion

| Positive indicators | Yes |
|---|:---:|
| Accepts personal responsibility for own decisions and actions. | ✓ |
| Takes action to resolve problems and fulfil own responsibilities. | ✓ |
| Keeps promises and does not let colleagues down. | |
| Takes pride in work. | ✓ |
| Is conscientious in completing work on time. | ✓ |
| Follows things through to satisfactory conclusion. | ✓ |
| Displays initiative, taking on tasks without having to be asked. | ✓ |
| Self-motivated, showing enthusiasm and dedication to their role. | ✓ |
| Focuses on task even if it is routine. | ✓ |

Improves own professional knowledge and keeps it up to date.

Is open, honest and genuine, standing up for what is right.

Makes decisions based upon ethical consideration and organisational integrity.    ✓

### *General observations*
1.   This account would fit equally within the core competencies of Effective communication and Personal responsibility

2.   The account takes care to describe what is happening and offers reasons behind the decisions made.

3.   Generally the structure follows SARA.

## Account 3 discussion

| Positive indicators | Yes |
|---|---|
| Accepts personal responsibility for own decisions and actions. | ✓ |
| Takes action to resolve problems and fulfil own responsibilities. | ✓ |
| Keeps promises and does not let colleagues down. | ✓ |
| Takes pride in work. | ✓ |
| Is conscientious in completing work on time. | ✓ |
| Follows things through to satisfactory conclusion. | ✓ |
| Displays initiative, taking on tasks without having to be asked. | ✓ |
| Self-motivated, showing enthusiasm and dedication to their role. | ✓ |
| Focuses on task even if it is routine. | |
| Improves own professional knowledge and keeps it up to date. | |
| Is open, honest and genuine, standing up for what is right. | ✓ |
| Makes decisions based upon ethical consideration and organisational integrity. | ✓ |

### *General observations*
1.   This scores very well against the positive indicators.

2.   It is well constructed but will still benefit from the use of SARA.

3.   The account follows a logical progression which is very much akin to telling a story.

# Personal responsibility and customer service

Personal responsibility, in this competency, refers to demonstrating good practice in the area of customer service, not your private life.

Finding suitable evidence for personal responsibility can be challenging, as some candidates mistake personal responsibility with doing all the work, thereby finding themselves with more 'personal responsibility' than they can deal with. In this competency it is linked to you providing appropriate customer service. It is easy to identify what people want from an organisation in relation to customer service; it is exactly what you would want from an organisation or company. The positive indicators above list many of these qualities. What tends to go wrong is that people's expectations are not met, in other words they do not get what they thought they should. In general terms people expect from a service provider:

- courtesy;
- smart appearance;
- quality and efficiency.

Courtesy is at the top of the list; if people feel someone has been rude to them, regardless of their own behaviour, they will complain. It is likely that within the assessment centre in the role plays, written exercises and perhaps via your interview accounts, you will be dealing with and referring to complaints. Taking personal responsibility for your actions means that you will always be thoughtful of others' feelings and be courteous at all times.

Being smartly dressed means that you are taking personal responsibility for ensuring the organisation is portrayed professionally. Further, if the quality or the efficiency of the service is let down by a department or individual, regardless of blame, then appropriate customer service means that you apologise for the situation. It is appropriate for you to state that you will take personal responsibility to ensure that the matter is dealt with properly and quickly.

Much of taking personal responsibility for things is a matter of common sense. Try not to become wrapped up in pointless arguments but deal with the issue. As with problem-solving, you cannot deal with the issue if you don't know what it is. If, after having identified the issue, you are unsure of the appropriate course of action to take at the time of dealing with a complaint or problem, ask yourself: If this person (the customer) was me, what outcome would I want from this conversation?

# Summary

This chapter has focused on the National Core Competency Personal responsibility, identifying the required level for the competency as well as the positive and negative indicators.

It has discussed example accounts, identifying strengths and areas which can be improved. Further, it has explained that the focus for personal responsibility in this competency is on customer service. Within the assessment centre you are likely to deal with complaints from customers. Remember to stay courteous at all times and to take personal responsibility to deal with the matter promptly.

# Further reading

Berne, E (1973) *Games People Play: The Psychology of Human Relationships*. London: Penguin

Harris, TA (1995) *I'm OK, You're OK*. London: Arrow

Stewart, I and Joines, V (1987) *TA Today. A New Introduction to Transactional Analysis*. Nottingham: Livespace

# Chapter 7
## Resilience

## Introduction

This chapter concentrates on the National Core Competency Resilience, identifying the required level for the competency as well as the positive and negative indicators. As in previous chapters, it discusses a number of accounts candidates have used during their interviews as examples. You are invited to identify which of the positive indicators are evident in the accounts and how they could be improved. Further, it discusses resilience in greater detail.

The competency Resilience is defined below.

*7. Resilience*
*Shows resilience, even in difficult circumstances. Prepared to make difficult decisions and has the confidence to see them through.*

The required level is as follows.

*Required level*
*Shows reliability and resilience in difficult circumstances. Remains calm and confident and responds logically and decisively in difficult situations.*

Further to the above are the positive indicators. These are a list of the behaviours that you will be expected to demonstrate during the assessment centre process (they have also been previously referred to as 'criteria'). During the assessment centre process you will be tested three times on each of the competencies. This means that you do not have to ensure that each of the positive indicators is addressed in every account. Further, although the indicators are considered during the interview, they also apply to other parts of the assessment centre process such as the interactive exercises and the written test.

### Positive indicators

- Is reliable in a crisis, remains calm and thinks clearly.

- Sorts out conflict and deals with hostility and provocation in a calm and restrained way.

- Responds to challenges rationally, avoiding inappropriate emotion.

- Deals with difficult emotional issues and then moves on.

- Manages conflicting pressures and tensions.
- Maintains professional ethics when confronted with pressure from others.
- Copes with ambiguity and deals with uncertainty and frustration.
- Resists pressure to make quick decisions where consideration is needed.
- Remains focused and in control of situation.
- Makes and carries through decisions, even though they are unpopular, difficult or controversial.
- Stands firmly by a position when it is right to do so.
- Defends their staff from excessive criticisms from outside the team.

## Negative indicators

A list of negative indicators identifies behaviour which is not wanted, as listed below.

- Gets easily upset, frustrated and annoyed.
- Panics and becomes agitated when problems arise.
- Walks away from confrontation when it would be more appropriate to get involved.
- Needs constant reassurance, support and supervision.
- Uses inappropriate physical force.
- Gets too emotionally involved in situations.
- Reacts inappropriately when faced with rude or abusive people.
- Deals with situations aggressively.
- Complains and whinges about problems rather than dealing with them.
- Gives in inappropriately when under pressure.
- Worries about making mistakes and avoids difficult situations wherever possible.

It is good practice to read through the negative indicators as they indicate exactly what you must not do. By changing the negative indicator to a positive statement you will ensure you are doing things in the correct way. For instance, negative indicator 'deals with situations aggressively', can be changed to 'deals with situations appropriately', which can be evidenced in your account.

# Account examples

The candidates were asked to:

*Describe to me when you have had to make a difficult decision.*

---

**TASK 1**

Consider the following three accounts and:

(a) Identify which of the positive indicators are demonstrated in each account.

(b) Think about how each could be improved.

(c) Note any other general observations you may have.

The positive indicators have been reproduced at the end of each account for your use and there is space for general observations.

Suggested answers are provided at the end of the chapter. However do be aware that here you are only assessing the written word and not a person in an interview situation.

---

# Account 1

*I am a black-belt chief instructor in the martial art form of Choi Kwang Do. During a martial art grading I was the examiner to a group of experienced pupils. It was evident from the start that one individual had not prepared; their technique and sequences were appalling. At the end of the exam I had no choice but to inform the individual of the failed exam. My martial art school has a reputation for passing students but I truly felt that I could not pass this one pupil.*

*It can be extremely upsetting failing an exam as many people do martial arts examinations as a group so that they progress onto the next level together. It also costs money to participate in an examination and so it can result in either an angry or upset individual. Overall it is never nice to be told you have failed.*

*I found it rather intimidating failing a pupil but the other examiners concurred with my judgement. It is also part of the responsibilities of a chief instructor, giving me no choice but to tell the bad news. It can be extremely embarrassing being told you have failed when you are being spoken to among the whole class.*

*I decided against following the traditional method of reading out the results at the end of examination and chose to speak to the pupil privately outside the hall while the remainder of the class were being warmed down. This way we would miss the read-out of results, saving the individual from sharing the bad news with the rest of the class. Once outside I told the pupil of the failed exam and that progress onto the next level would not be allowed. I explained the result taking into account the fact that I had to be compassionate about the failure but also making clear that I still held the respect and discipline of a chief instructor. I didn't want the pupil to feel too upset so I offered to help them to achieve the required standard by offering personal teaching at the end of each lesson.*

*I knew I would receive some criticism from a number of people for failing the individual. I didn't want this to alter my train of thought and affect my morals when it comes to my responsibility of being an instructor.*

| Positive indicators | Yes |
|---|---|
| Is reliable in a crisis, remains calm and thinks clearly. | |
| Sorts out conflict and deals with hostility and provocation in a calm and restrained way. | |
| Responds to challenges rationally, avoiding inappropriate emotion. | |
| Deals with difficult emotional issues and then moves on. | |
| Manages conflicting pressures and tensions. | |
| Maintains professional ethics when confronted with pressure from others. | |
| Copes with ambiguity and deals with uncertainty and frustration. | |
| Resists pressure to make quick decisions where consideration is needed. | |
| Remains focused and in control of situation. | |
| Makes and carries through decisions, even though they are unpopular, difficult or controversial. | |
| Stands firmly by a position when it is right to do so. | |
| Defends their staff from excessive criticisms from outside the team. | |

## *General observations*

# Account 2

During my voluntary work I was given a 14-year-old student to mentor. The student had Asperger's syndrome and had been referred to us by the school as there were anger management issues. During the first few months it became apparent that these bouts of anger were a result of being teased and taunted by peers. The student also became a regular attendee of our youth club where I was working, and was liked and respected by the other young people who, while they were aware of the condition, found the student kind, thoughtful and very amusing. When we were deciding on a new member of the team to be picked from the young people, I suggested my mentee and this was agreed. The student was delighted and excited at the prospect of being given responsibility and respect.

One evening soon after, I was informed prior to the session that another youngster had been suggested who didn't have any anger issues and the team felt this person would be more reliable within the youth club. I was shocked and disappointed that there had been a change of decision within the team without my being consulted. I challenged the members immediately, reminding them of the ethos of the group – that all individuals be treated as equal with no prejudging. It appeared that the school report, claiming the student to be volatile, had been raised and concern expressed for the other young people. I argued that this was unfair and a weak justification for the change of plan as the report had been written when the student was being bullied and because of the Asperger's had been unable to express feelings properly and too much had been assumed. I stated that a meeting must be held so that I could present the case clearly and rationally and I wanted the student to be able to attend. We agreed that this would take place after the club that night. This would give me time to put a case together and not let feelings of anger or frustration cloud my judgement.

I had to tell the student of the proposals and initially it was extremely distressing. The student tried to run away from the club and thumped the door. When I pointed out that behaving like this was only making the case worse, confirming my colleagues' thoughts, the student calmed down and was able to listen to me. I wanted the student to speak at the meeting about the enjoyment of coming to the club, helping other young people.

After the meeting the team were still not convinced. I assured the student I would do my very best to find a solution that would make everyone happy. The team felt that the student would not be able to focus on the other young people and their problems because of not being able to see another person's viewpoint. I suggested that the only way to find this out was to try it and see. I told them that I would accept full responsibility and pointed out that an adult was always in every room with the *youngsters so we would see if anything happened and be able to intervene. I stressed what a huge beneficial effect this would have from the point of view of confidence and self-esteem and I felt sure the student would be able to make some friends within the group in this role. Also, telling someone one week that they could do the job then telling them the next that they are no longer needed was unfair and extremely unkind. I felt that the only people benefitting from the change of mind were the team, as the other candidate had few behaviour problems so would make it easier for us. I controlled my temper and frustration at all times and remained focused on the issue in hand. I felt isolated from the team and very disappointed, but I detailed the student's attributes and reasons for appointment in a calm, logical manner. I was not afraid to stand up against the other members of the team as I knew this was of huge importance to the youngster's development. I felt the student was being discriminated against because of the Asperger's.*

*I suggested that we take both young people on as helpers as it would only be an advantage to the team to have more helpers working with them. The team agreed to try it. I thanked them all and told them they would all be pleasantly surprised at how much my mentee was capable of. I felt delighted and telephoned to give him the good news.*

*It worked very well. There was the odd occasion where the student was not as focused on the other young people as would have been expected but on the whole the set-up worked amazingly well. The student became confident, was proud, and talked openly about Asperger's to the other youngsters, which helped them come to terms with some of their issues.*

*I managed to keep my disappointment under control and focus on the important issue – the well-being of the student. I wouldn't let anyone tell me otherwise. I came up with a solution which meant that neither young person was disappointed and the team were able to agree.*

---

**Positive indicators**                                                      **Yes**

Is reliable in a crisis, remains calm and thinks clearly.

Sorts out conflict and deals with hostility and provocation in a calm
and restrained way.

Responds to challenges rationally, avoiding inappropriate emotion.

Deals with difficult emotional issues and then moves on.

Manages conflicting pressures and tensions.

Maintains professional ethics when confronted with pressure from
others.

Copes with ambiguity and deals with uncertainty and frustration.

Resists pressure to make quick decisions where consideration is needed.

Remains focused and in control of situation.

Makes and carries through decisions, even though they are unpopular, difficult or controversial.

Stands firmly by a position when it is right to do so.

Defends their staff from excessive criticisms from outside the team.

*General observations*

# Account 3

*In my spare time I enjoy horse riding. When I was in my early teens I would ride on a regular basis. I would also attend various competitions, jumping, showing, cross-country, etc. On one occasion I was very nervous before a show-jumping class. I went into the school and jumped the first few jumps clear. I came up to my fourth jump and the horse refused and I fell over his head. I landed on my head and knocked myself unconscious. The last thing I remember was waking up in an ambulance to a paramedic asking me if I was OK. I hadn't suffered any injuries luckily but was very shaken up and wobbly on my feet. I remember saying to my instructor that I did not want to ride again. I was affected by this experience and lost a lot of confidence riding a horse. My instructor, my family and friends told me it was important to get back onto a horse, as I might not want to ride again and it would be a great loss. A few days later I returned to the stables to see the horse. I was then told I would have to get back on the horse. With a lot of thought and not wanting to, I decided I would get back on as I had a lot to lose if I didn't. I was apprehensive and nervous when I got back on the horse. I became upset and was frightened. After several minutes I calmed down and thought 'I am going to have to ride my horse again, and I can't let a knock-back affect me'. Several days later I returned to the stables and rode again, this time jumping small cross-poles; this took a lot of courage. I then decided I would show-jump again at the same show and this time complete the course. So I returned to the show a few months later and completed the course and came first. It was the greatest feeling, not just that I had won but also because I had shown resilience and got back onto the horse and decided to show-jump again.*

| Positive indicators | Yes |
|---|---|
| Is reliable in a crisis, remains calm and thinks clearly. | |
| Sorts out conflict and deals with hostility and provocation in a calm and restrained way. | |
| Responds to challenges rationally, avoiding inappropriate emotion. | |
| Deals with difficult emotional issues and then moves on. | |
| Manages conflicting pressures and tensions. | |
| Maintains professional ethics when confronted with pressure from others. | |

Copes with ambiguity and deals with uncertainty and frustration.

Resists pressure to make quick decisions where consideration is needed.

Remains focused and in control of situation.

Makes and carries through decisions, even though they are unpopular, difficult or controversial.

Stands firmly by a position when it is right to do so.

Defends their staff from excessive criticisms from outside the team.

### General observations

# Account 1 discussion

| Positive indicators | Yes |
|---|---|
| Is reliable in a crisis, remains calm and thinks clearly. | |
| Sorts out conflict and deals with hostility and provocation in a calm and restrained way. | |
| Responds to challenges rationally, avoiding inappropriate emotion. | |
| Deals with difficult emotional issues and then moves on. | |
| Manages conflicting pressures and tensions. | ✓ |
| Maintains professional ethics when confronted with pressure from others. | ✓ |
| Copes with ambiguity and deals with uncertainty and frustration. | |
| Resists pressure to make quick decisions where consideration is needed. | |
| Remains focused and in control of situation. | ✓ |
| Makes and carries through decisions, even though they are unpopular, difficult or controversial. | ✓ |
| Stands firmly by a position when it is right to do so. | ✓ |
| Defends their staff from excessive criticisms from outside the team. | |

### General observations

1. In general the choice of topic is suitable for the question asked.
2. The introduction enabled the listener to understand the situation.
3. This might have benefitted from a description of how the recipient was affected by the news; doing this might have meant that further competencies could be met.

# Account 2 discussion

| Positive indicators | Yes |
|---|---|
| Is reliable in a crisis, remains calm and thinks clearly. | |
| Sorts out conflict and deals with hostility and provocation in a calm and restrained way. | ✓ |
| Responds to challenges rationally, avoiding inappropriate emotion. | ✓ |
| Deals with difficult emotional issues and then moves on. | ✓ |
| Manages conflicting pressures and tensions. | ✓ |
| Maintains professional ethics when confronted with pressure from others. | ✓ |
| Copes with ambiguity and deals with uncertainty and frustration. | |
| Resists pressure to make quick decisions where consideration is needed. | |

| | |
|---|---|
| Remains focused and in control of situation. | ✓ |
| Makes and carries through decisions, even though they are unpopular, difficult or controversial. | ✓ |
| Stands firmly by a position when it is right to do so. | ✓ |
| Defends their staff from excessive criticisms from outside the team. | ✓ |

### *General observations*

1. This account is very strong. The reason for this is the detail that is expressed, and as a result it scores well against the competencies.

2. SARA is alluded to, in fact the situation, actions and results were repeated as the account evolved.

3. This account could be used for the competency Respect for race and diversity, where an individual with a learning difficulty is being treated less fairly than others.

4. The account of actually challenging the above treatment was most appropriate.

## Account 3 discussion

| **Positive indicators** | **Yes** |
|---|---|
| Is reliable in a crisis, remains calm and thinks clearly. | |
| Sorts out conflict and deals with hostility and provocation in a calm and restrained way. | |
| Responds to challenges rationally, avoiding inappropriate emotion. | |
| Deals with difficult emotional issues and then moves on. | ✓ |
| Manages conflicting pressures and tensions. | ✓ |
| Maintains professional ethics when confronted with pressure from others. | |
| Copes with ambiguity and deals with uncertainty and frustration. | |
| Resists pressure to make quick decisions where consideration is needed. | |
| Remains focused and in control of situation. | ✓ |
| Makes and carries through decisions, even though they are unpopular, difficult or controversial. | |
| Stands firmly by a position when it is right to do so. | |
| Defends their staff from excessive criticisms from outside the team. | |

### *General observations*

1. This account is a great explanation of personal resilience, exhibiting the difficulties faced following a riding accident.

2.  It does not score well against the competencies for the simple fact that the account included only one individual. As a result any tensions indicated in the competency were not met.

3.  This highlights the importance of selecting the most appropriate account. This can only be achieved if a number of accounts are available for selection in the first instance.

# Resilience

Demonstrating resilience is not always easy; doing the right thing in the face of adversity is seldom popular with those you are dealing with at the time. The main problem faced by candidates is that to exhibit resilience, you have to first know that what you are doing is correct, before sticking to that course of action.

It is useful to consider situations in their social context. There are occasions when things around you can change, sometimes before you really notice what has happened exactly.

---

**TASK 2**

Read the following scenario and explain how the situation changed.

*You are walking through a shopping centre and a man and a woman are arguing. You think nothing much of it but the shouting becomes louder and the man threatens to hit the woman. By now you are quite close by and feel that if you don't intervene, someone is going to get hurt. You approach the man and suggest that he stops what he is doing immediately. You are abused by the man, who suggests you go away, and he threatens to punch you. You move away slightly and call the police on your mobile. The woman is absolutely infuriated. 'How dare you?!' she shouts.*

*The abuse is now aimed at you.*

---

You tried to help the woman and now she has turned against you; you are the 'bad' one. This situation is sometimes referred to as the 'drama triangle', originally from the concept of Eric Berne in the 1950s. The following occurs: sometimes we, unconsciously, take on roles. In the situation above there were three: persecutor, victim and rescuer.

The persecutor attacks the victim and you rescue the victim, doing the 'right' thing. Next things change. The persecutor has become the victim, you have become the persecutor and the once victim now feels the need to rescue the [new] victim from you.

> **TASK 3**
>
> Explain how resilience can be demonstrated in the following scenario.
>
> *A parent makes a complaint to the police about other parents parking on the yellow zig-zag line outside a school, making crossing the road dangerous. A child nearly had an accident. A police officer is sent to the school, finds cars parked on the yellow line and starts writing out a parking ticket. Next, parents shout abuse at the police officer; they are only there for two minutes to drop off their child; hasn't the officer got criminals to catch?*

As before, the rescuer (the police officer) has become the persecutor, handing out parking tickets to the innocent victims (parents). The police officer could be tempted to be sympathetic to the parents, maybe finding it difficult to park near school, dropping off children themselves. However, to demonstrate resilience you have to stick to what you know to be the right thing, not being persuaded to act differently. Despite the protests of the parents, calling the officer names, the officer carries on with the tickets, thereby showing resilience.

The roles people adopt are many more than have been used in the examples. They can include the joker, expert, likeable rogue, simpleton, brainy, etc. These roles are decided prior to your arrival. Upon your arrival they can change immediately. However, regardless of the roles people choose to play, there are times when you have to be quite hard, not giving in to pleas, but sticking to what you know to be right. Remember, it is of vital importance that what you are sticking to is indeed what is right.

As you look for suitable accounts for your interviews, consider the roles people adopt and what can happen when they change. Consider then what is required of you to show resilience.

# Summary

This chapter has focused on the National Core Competency Resilience, identifying the required level for the competency as well as the positive and negative indicators.

It has discussed example accounts, identifying strengths and areas which can be improved. Further, it has discussed resilience, explaining different roles people can adopt, and how you need to stick to what you know is the right thing to do.

# Further reading

If you are interested in reading more about this and similar subjects, consider the following books.

Berne, E (1973) *Games People Play: The Psychology of Human Relationships*. London: Penguin

Harris, TA (1995) *I'm OK, You're OK*. London: Arrow

Stewart, I and Joines, V (1987) *TA Today. A New Introduction to Transactional Analysis*. Nottingham: Livespace

# Chapter 8
## Creating your own accounts

## Introduction

The previous chapters concentrated on the interview process, describing all seven core competencies, identifying the required level, as well as the positive and negative indicators. For each competency three example accounts have been discussed, indicating strengths, areas for improvement and general observations.

This chapter supports you in writing your own accounts. It provides a framework, suggests how to organise the accounts and emphasises the importance of reflective practice. Remember, the accounts should contain only your own experiences; you cannot 'borrow' any material from this book.

## Framework for your accounts

In the introduction to the book you were asked to bullet point an idea for each of the core competencies. Return to these, or consider alternatives if you want to change your ideas after reading the previous chapters.

|      | Title                          | 1 | 2 | 3 |
|------|--------------------------------|---|---|---|
| Ch 1 | Respect for race and diversity |   |   |   |
| Ch 2 | Teamworking                    |   |   |   |
| Ch 3 | Community and customer focus   |   |   |   |
| Ch 4 | Effective communication        |   |   |   |
| Ch 5 | Problem-solving                |   |   |   |
| Ch 6 | Personal responsibility        |   |   |   |
| Ch 7 | Resilience                     |   |   |   |

# Respect for race and diversity

---

**TASK 1**

Using the steps below, consider Respect for race and diversity.

**Step 1** Identify a question

**Step 2** Consider a suitable answer

**Step 3** Write the account in full

It is suggested that you use a separate piece of paper or a computer.

**Step 4** Compare and contrast

How does the account compare against the positive indicators?

---

**Positive indicators**                                                    **Yes**

Sees issues from other people's viewpoints.

Is polite, tolerant and patient with people inside and outside the organisation, treating them with respect and dignity.

Respects the needs of everyone involved when sorting out disagreements.

Shows understanding and sensitivity to people's problems and vulnerabilities.

Deals with diversity issues and gives positive practical support to staff who may feel vulnerable.

Listens to and values others' views and opinions.

Uses language in an appropriate way and is sensitive to the way it may affect people.

Acknowledges and respects a broad range of social and cultural customs and beliefs and values within the law.

Understands what offends others and adapts own actions accordingly.

Respects and maintains confidentiality, where appropriate.

Delivers difficult messages sensitively.

Challenges attitudes and behaviour which are abusive, aggressive or discriminatory.

Takes into account others' personal needs and interests.

Supports minority groups both inside and outside their organisation.

### Step 5 Rehearsal

Talk through your account until you can do so without forgetting any important elements.

### Step 6 Timings

Aim to get as close as possible to the five minutes allocated.

### Step 7 Practise

Practise for as long as you need to to get the retelling of your account almost word-perfect.

# Team working

---

**TASK 2**

Using the steps below, consider Teamworking.

**Step 1** Identify a question

**Step 2** Consider a suitable answer

**Step 3** Write the account in full

It is suggested that you use a separate piece of paper or a computer.

**Step 4** Compare and contrast

How does the account compare against the positive indicators?

---

**Positive indicators**                                                      **Yes**

Understands own role in a team.

Actively supports and assists the team to reach their objectives.

Is approachable and friendly to others.

Makes time to get to know people.

Co-operates with and supports others.

Offers to help other people.

Asks for and accepts help when needed.

Develops mutual trust and confidence in others.

---

Willingly takes on unpopular or routine tasks.

Contributes to team objectives no matter what the direct personal benefit may be.

Acknowledges that there is often a need to be a member of more than one team.

Takes pride in their team and promotes their team's performance to others.

**Step 5** Rehearsal

Talk through your account until you can do so without forgetting any important elements.

**Step 6** Timings

Aim to get as close as possible to the five minutes allocated.

**Step 7** Practise

Practise for as long as you need to to get the retelling of your account almost word-perfect.

# Community and customer focus

---

**TASK 3**

Using the steps below, consider Community and customer focus.

**Step 1** Identify a question

**Step 2** Consider a suitable answer

**Step 3** Write the account in full

It is suggested that you use a separate piece of paper or a computer.

**Step 4** Compare and contrast

How does the account compare against the positive indicators?

---

**Positive indicators**                                                     **Yes**

Presents an appropriate image to the public and other organisations.

Supports strategies that aim to build an organisation that reflects the community it serves.

Focuses on the customer in all activities.

Tries to sort out customers' problems as quickly as possible.

Apologises when they are at fault or have made mistakes.

Responds quickly to customer requests.

Makes sure that customers are satisfied with the service they receive.

Manages customer expectations.

Keeps customers updated on progress.

Balances customer needs with organisational needs.

**Step 5** Rehearsal

Talk through your account until you can do so without forgetting any important elements.

**Step 6** Timings

Aim to get as close as possible to the five minutes allocated.

**Step 7** Practise

Practise for as long as you need to to get the retelling of your account almost word-perfect.

# Effective communication

---

**TASK 4**

Using the steps below, consider Effective communication.

**Step 1** Identify a question

**Step 2** Consider a suitable answer

**Step 3** Write the account in full

It is suggested that you use a separate piece of paper or a computer.

**Step 4** Compare and contrast

How does the account compare against the positive indicators?

---

**Positive indicators**                                                     **Yes**

Deals with issues directly.

Clearly communicates needs and instructions.

Clearly communicates management decisions and policy, and the reasons behind them.

Communicates face-to-face wherever possible and if appropriate.

Speaks with authority and confidence.

Changes the style of communication to meet the needs of the audience.

Manages group discussions effectively.

Summarises information to check people understand it.

Supports arguments and recommendations effectively in writing.

Produces well-structured reports and written summaries.

**Step 5** Rehearsal

Talk through your account until you can do so without forgetting any important elements.

**Step 6** Timings

Aim to get as close as possible to the five minutes allocated.

**Step 7** Practise

Practise for as long as you need to to get the retelling of your account almost word-perfect.

# Problem-solving

---

**TASK 5**

Using the steps below, consider Problem-solving.

**Step 1** Identify a question

**Step 2** Consider a suitable answer

**Step 3** Write the account in full

It is suggested that you use a separate piece of paper or a computer.

**Step 4** Compare and contrast

How does the account compare against the positive indicators?

---

| **Positive indicators** | **Yes** |
| --- | --- |
| Identifies where to get information and gets it. | |
| Gets as much information as is appropriate on all respects of a problem. | |
| Separates relevant information from irrelevant information and important information from unimportant information. | |
| Takes on information quickly and accurately. | |
| Reviews all the information gathered to understand the situation and to draw logical conclusions. | |
| Identifies and links causes and effects. | |

Identifies what can and cannot be changed.

Takes a systematic approach to solving problems.

Remains impartial and avoids jumping to conclusions.

Refers to procedures and precedents, as necessary, before making decisions.

Makes good decisions that take account of all relevant factors.

**Step 5** Rehearsal

Talk through your account until you can do so without forgetting any important elements.

**Step 6** Timings

Aim to get as close as possible to the five minutes allocated.

**Step 7** Practise

Practise for as long as you need to to get the retelling of your account almost word-perfect.

# Personal responsibility

---

**TASK 6**

Using the steps below, consider Personal responsibility.

**Step 1** Identify a question

**Step 2** Consider a suitable answer

**Step 3** Write the account in full

It is suggested that you use a separate piece of paper or a computer.

**Step 4** Compare and contrast

How does the account compare against the positive indicators?

---

| **Positive indicators** | **Yes** |
| --- | --- |
| Accepts personal responsibility for own decisions and actions. | |
| Takes action to resolve problems and fulfil own responsibilities. | |
| Keeps promises and does not let colleagues down. | |
| Takes pride in work. | |
| Is conscientious in completing work on time. | |
| Follows things through to satisfactory conclusion. | |
| Displays initiative, taking on tasks without having to be asked. | |
| Self-motivated, showing enthusiasm and dedication to their role. | |

Focuses on task even if it is routine.

Improves own professional knowledge and keeps it up to date.

Is open, honest and genuine, standing up for what is right.

Makes decisions based upon ethical consideration and organisational integrity.

**Step 5** Rehearsal

Talk through your account until you can do so without forgetting any important elements.

**Step 6** Timings

Aim to get as close as possible to the five minutes allocated.

**Step 7** Practise

Practise for as long as you need to to get the retelling of your account almost word-perfect.

# Resilience

---

**TASK 7**

Using the steps below, consider Resilience.

**Step 1** Identify a question

**Step 2** Consider a suitable answer

**Step 3** Write the account in full

It is suggested that you use a separate piece of paper or a computer.

**Step 4** Compare and contrast

How does the account compare against the positive indicators?

---

| **Positive indicators** | **Yes** |
|---|---|
| Is reliable in a crisis, remains calm and thinks clearly. | |
| Sorts out conflict and deals with hostility and provocation in a calm and restrained way. | |
| Responds to challenges rationally, avoiding inappropriate emotion. | |
| Deals with difficult emotional issues and then moves on. | |
| Manages conflicting pressures and tensions. | |
| Maintains professional ethics when confronted with pressure from others. | |
| Copes with ambiguity and deals with uncertainty and frustration. | |

Resists pressure to make quick decisions where consideration is needed.

Remains focused and in control of situation.

Makes and carries through decisions, even though they are unpopular, difficult or controversial.

Stands firmly by a position when it is right to do so.

Defends their staff from excessive criticisms from outside the team.

**Step 5** Rehearsal

Talk through your account until you can do so without forgetting any important elements.

**Step 6** Timings

Aim to get as close as possible to the five minutes allocated.

**Step 7** Practise

Practise for as long as you need to to get the retelling of your account almost word-perfect.

You now have seven accounts, one for each core competency. Aim to have three accounts for each competency, so that no matter what question you are asked, you have an answer. Therefore, go through the process again. If you have used work examples only, consider using examples from other aspects of your life, such as hobbies, home life, social life, voluntary work, etc.

# Organisation

You now have a total of 21 examples to draw from. How are you going to remember them? Most people remember best by association: coding the information so that it can easily be retrieved from the memory. Different coding strategies can be used. You can use any strategy that suits you. One that seems to work for many is to link each account to a finger or toe (with 21 you will have to use your nose too). Look at your hands and decide which competency is going on which finger. Do the same for your toes. Finally place the last one on your nose. Now you have your own filing system and can call upon any of your accounts at will.

Other people colour-code each of the competencies to differentiate their accounts in combination with numbers 1, 2 and 3. Another method is to just use a combination of numbers:

1:3 represents Respect for race and diversity (competency 1), third account

5:1 is Problem solving (competency 5), first account.

Use what works for you.

# Reflective practice

As you prepare your interview accounts, it is good practice to involve a critical friend. This could be a friend, colleague or member of your family who will listen to you and provide feedback on your account. Discuss the following.

- How many positive indicators are met?

- Did the account take the required five minutes?

- Your :

- body language

- tone of voice

- use of inflections

- use of language.

- Did you sound convincing or contrived?

- Did they understand what you were describing?

To complement this feedback it is useful to engage in reflective practice. After you have taken part in a mock interview and received feedback from your critical friend, take some time to think about your performance. Ask yourself four questions.

## 1. What did I do?

You relive the interview thinking about what you did. Reliving the experience enables you to consider what actually happened. The recall of your own experience will probably differ from that of the person interviewing you. You will benefit from being as honest as you can. You recall whether you actually covered all the significant parts of your account.

## 2. How well did I do it?

Only you really know how well you did, whether you struggled to remember the account, find the words or found it difficult to vocalise some of the sentences. At this stage you think about your interview account and ask yourself the following.

- How well did I use the time?
- How was my body language?
- How was the structure of my account?
- Do I feel that I struggle with any particular words?
- Can I remember all of the prepared accounts?

The difference between question 1 and question 2 of the process is that at question 1 you recall whether or not you included all the salient parts. In question 2 you ask yourself how well you did it.

## 3. What guidance does this book offer?

Ask the following.

- Does this account actually answer the question?
- Am I happy with this account?
- Is there anything in the back of my mind that I am ignoring?

Refer to the appropriate chapter and check that your written account and the parts that you have ad-libbed as you embellished the account, are appropriate and match the criteria.

## 4. What will I do differently in future?

You are best placed to answer this: you have thought about what happened, reflected upon how you did and referred back to the salient chapter of this book to identify what else you could have included.

# Next, devise an action plan

An action plan is a statement of intention enabling you to achieve a specific outcome or goal. A goal is more likely to be realised if you first think about what you want to achieve, break it down into its component parts and then show determination to achieve that goal. What you are doing is taking responsibility for your own actions and wishes. If you identify your own goals, rather than following the advice of someone else, you are more likely to achieve that goal. Some people procrastinate, they partake in activities that are more fun or which involve less effort. To draw up an action plan takes little effort, it is the 'action' that takes the effort.

Action plans should be SMART. That means they should be:

- Specific.

- Measurable.

- Achievable.

- Relevant.

- Timed.

---

**TASK 8**

Look at the example action plan; write one for an area you want to develop.

Example action plan:

Desired outcome – To obtain more examples for the competency Effective communication

---

### Action plan

**Specific**
To obtain more examples for the competency Effective communication by volunteering for work at the local charity shop. I anticipate assisting a wide range of customers

**Measurable**
To collate at least three quality examples for my assessment interview

**Achievable**
This is achievable if I pay attention to my interactions with customers and record them soon after the event

**Relevant**
This is relevant to the interviews within the assessment centre

**Timed**
To be completed within two months

---

The form below can be used to record your observations.

| Reflective practice sheet | |
|---|---|
| **Title** | **Your observations** |
| 1. What did I do? | |
| 2. How well did I do it? | |
| 3. What guidance does this book offer? | |
| 4. What will I do differently in future? | Desired outcome: |
| 5. Action plan | S<br>M<br>A<br>R<br>T |

*Reflective practice is all about taking responsibility for your own efforts in an attempt to improve whatever it is you are doing. You are the person who knows best what you can do well and what needs improving, so arguably it is you who is best placed to decide what requires improvement.*

(Malthouse, Kennard and Roffey-Barentsen, 2009)

Advice from other people, such as a critical friend, will of course be useful. However, they will approach any feedback from their own perspective, not yours. According to Malthouse, Kennard and Roffey-Barentsen (2009), these factors include:

- how you felt at the time;

- what you were thinking;

- what you were not thinking;

- what you found most difficult;

- how it was for you, etc.

Only you are conscious of these considerations and only you can decide exactly how and what you are going to do that will best improve what you are doing. Reflective practice is something which is informed by you, because only you know what your areas for development are. *The process of reflective practice is a very personal one. The great thing about it is that it actually works. To make it work for you, you must first be honest with yourself and listen to your own advice.* (Malthouse, Kennard and Raffey-Barentsen, 2009)

# Summary

This chapter has supported you in writing your own accounts by providing a framework with easy-to-follow steps. It has discussed strategies for organising the accounts to make them memorable. Further, it has emphasised the importance of reflective practice, as only you can tell how well you have done and how your accounts can be improved.

# References

Malthouse, R., Kennard, P and Roffey-Barentsen, J (2009) *Interactive Exercises for the Police Recruit Assessment Process: Succeeding at Role Plays.* Exeter: Learning Matters

# Appendix

## National Core Competencies

Reproduced in part, with kind permission, from *The Integrated Competency Behavioural Framework Version 9.0 (May 2007)* by Skills for Justice.

**1. Respect for race and diversity** — Considers and shows respect for the opinions, circumstances and feelings of colleagues and members of the public, no matter what their race, religion, position, background, circumstances, status or appearance.

**Required level** — Understands other people's views and takes them into account. Is tactful and diplomatic when dealing with people. Treats them with dignity and respect at all times. Understands and is sensitive to social, cultural and racial differences.

- Sees issues from other people's viewpoints.

- Is polite, tolerant and patient with people inside and outside the organisation, treating them with respect and dignity.

- Respects the needs of everyone involved when sorting out disagreements.

- Shows understanding and sensitivity to people's problems and vulnerabilities.

- Deals with diversity issues and gives positive practical support to staff who may feel vulnerable.

- Listens to and values others' views and opinions.

- Uses language in an appropriate way and is sensitive to the way it may affect people.

- Acknowledges and respects a broad range of social and cultural customs and beliefs and values within the law.

- Understands what offends others and adapts own actions accordingly.

- Respects and maintains confidentiality, where appropriate.

- Delivers difficult messages sensitively.

- Challenges attitudes and behaviour which are abusive, aggressive or discriminatory.

- Takes into account others' personal needs and interests.

- Supports minority groups both inside and outside their organisation.

**Negative indicators**

- Does not consider other people's feelings.

- Does not encourage people to talk about personal issues.

- Criticises people without considering their feelings and motivation.

- Makes situations worse with inappropriate remarks, language or behaviour.

- Is thoughtless and tactless when dealing with people.

- Is dismissive and impatient with people.

- Does not respect confidentiality.

- Unnecessarily emphasises power and control in situations where this is not appropriate.

- Intimidates others in an aggressive and overpowering way.

- Uses humour inappropriately.

- Shows bias and prejudice when dealing with people.

| | |
|---|---|
| **2. Team working** | Develops strong working relationships inside and outside the team to achieve common goals. Breaks down barriers between groups and involves others in discussions and decisions. |
| **Required level** | Works effectively as a team member and helps build relationships within it. Actively helps and supports others to achieve team goals. |

- Understands own role in a team.

- Actively supports and assists the team to reach their objectives.

- Is approachable and friendly to others.

- Makes time to get to know people.

- Co-operates with and supports others.

- Offers to help other people.

- Asks for and accepts help when needed.

- Develops mutual trust and confidence in others.

- Willingly takes on unpopular or routine tasks.

- Contributes to team objectives no matter what the direct personal benefit may be.

- Acknowledges that there is often a need to be a member of more than one team.

- Takes pride in their team and promotes their team's performance to others.

**Negative indicators**

- Does not volunteer to help other team members.

- Is only interested in taking part in high-profile and interesting activities.

- Takes credit for success without recognising the contribution of others.

- Works to own agenda rather than contributing to team performance.

- Allows small exclusive groups of people to develop.

- Plays one person off against another.

- Restricts and controls what information is shared.

- Does not let people say what they think.

- Does not offer advice or get advice from others.

- Shows little interest in working jointly with other groups to meet the goals of everyone involved.

- Does not discourage conflict within the organisation.

| | |
|---|---|
| **3. Community and customer focus** | Focuses on the customer and provides a high-quality service that is tailored to meet their individual needs. Understands the communities that are served and shows an active commitment to policing that reflects their needs and concerns. |
| **Required level** | Provides a high level of service to customers. Maintains contact with customers, works out what they need and responds to them. |

- Presents an appropriate image to the public and other organisations.

- Supports strategies that aim to build an organisation that reflects the community it serves.

- Focuses on the customer in all activities.

- Tries to sort out customers' problems as quickly as possible.

- Apologises when they are at fault or have made mistakes.

- Responds quickly to customer requests.

- Makes sure that customers are satisfied with the service they receive.

- Manages customer expectations.

- Keeps customers updated on progress.

- Balances customer needs with organisational needs.

## Negative indicators

- Is not customer focused and does not consider individual needs.

- Does not tell customers what is going on.

- Presents an unprofessional image to customers.

- Only sees a situation from their own view, not from the customer's view.

- Shows little interest in the customer – only deals with their immediate problem.

- Does not respond to the needs of the local community.

- Focuses on organisational issues rather than customer needs.

- Does not make the most of opportunities to talk to people in the community.

- Slow to respond to customers' requests.

- Fails to check that the customers' needs have been met.

| | |
|---|---|
| **4. Effective communication** | Communicates ideas and information effectively, both verbally and in writing. Uses language and a style of communication that is appropriate to the situation and people being addressed. Makes sure others understand what is going on. |
| **Required level** | Communicates all needs, instructions and decisions clearly. Adapts the style of communication to meet the needs of the audience. Checks for understanding. |

- Deals with issues directly.

- Clearly communicates needs and instructions.

- Clearly communicates management decisions and policy, and the reasons behind them.

- Communicates face to face wherever possible and if appropriate.

- Speaks with authority and confidence.

- Changes the style of communication to meet the needs of the audience.

- Manages group discussions effectively.

- Summarises information to check people understand it.

- Supports arguments and recommendations effectively in writing.

- Produces well-structured reports and written summaries.

## Negative indicators

- Is hesitant, nervous and uncertain when speaking.

- Speaks without first thinking through what to say.

- Uses inappropriate language or jargon.

- Speaks in a rambling way.

- Does not consider the target audience.

- Avoids answering difficult questions.

- Does not give full information without being questioned.

- Writes in an unstructured way.

- Uses poor spelling, punctuation and grammar.

- Assumes others understand what has been said without actually checking.

- Does not listen and interrupts at inappropriate times.

**5. Problem solving**   Gathers information from a range of sources. Analyses information to identify problems and issues and makes effective decisions.

**Required level**   Gathers enough relevant information to understand specific issues and events. Uses information to identify problems and draw conclusions. Makes good decisions.

- Identifies where to get information and gets it.

- Gets as much information as is appropriate on all aspects of a problem.

- Separates relevant information from irrelevant information and important information from unimportant information.

- Takes on information quickly and accurately.

- Reviews all the information gathered to understand the situation and to draw logical conclusions.

- Identifies and links causes and effects.

- Identifies what can and cannot be changed.

- Takes a systematic approach to solving problems.

- Remains impartial and avoids jumping to conclusions.

- Refers to procedures and precedents, as necessary, before making decisions.

- Makes good decisions that take account of all relevant factors.

**Negative indicators**

- Doesn't deal with problems in detail and does not identify underlying issues.

- Does not gather enough information before coming to conclusions.

- Does not consult other people who may have extra information.

- Does not research background.

- Shows no interest in gathering or using intelligence.
- Does not gather evidence.
- Makes assumptions about the facts of a situation.
- Does not recognise problems until they have become significant issues.
- Gets stuck in the detail of complex situations and cannot see the main issues.
- Reacts without considering all the angles.
- Becomes distracted by minor issues.

**6. Personal responsibility**   Takes personal responsibility for making things happen and achieving results. Displays motivation, commitment, perseverance and conscientiousness. Acts with a high degree of integrity.

**Required level**   Takes personal responsibility for own actions and for sorting out issues or problems that arise. Is focused on achieving results to required standards and developing skills and knowledge.

- Accepts personal responsibility for own decisions and actions.
- Takes action to resolve problems and fulfil own responsibilities.
- Keeps promises and does not let colleagues down.
- Takes pride in work.
- Is conscientious in completing work on time.
- Follows things through to satisfactory conclusion.
- Displays initiative, taking on tasks without having to be asked.
- Is self-motivated, showing enthusiasm and dedication to their role.
- Focuses on task even if it is routine.
- Improves own professional knowledge and keeps it up to date.
- Is open, honest and genuine, standing up for what is right.
- Makes decisions based upon ethical consideration and organisational integrity.

**Negative indicators**

- Passes responsibility upwards inappropriately.
- Is not concerned about letting others down.
- Will not deal with issues, just hopes they will go away.
- Blames others rather than admitting to mistakes or looking for help.

- Is unwilling to take on responsibility.
- Puts in the minimum effort that is needed to get by.
- Shows a negative and disruptive attitude.
- Shows little energy and enthusiasm for work.
- Expresses a cynical attitude to the organisation and their job.
- Gives up easily when faced with problems.
- Fails to recognise personal weaknesses and development needs.
- Makes little or no attempt to develop self or keep up to date.

**7. Resilience**  Shows resilience, even in difficult circumstances. Is prepared to make difficult decisions and has the confidence to see them through.

**Required level**  Shows reliability and resilience in difficult circumstances. Remains calm and confident and responds logically and decisively in difficult situations.

- Is reliable in a crisis, remains calm and thinks clearly.
- Sorts out conflict and deals with hostility and provocation in a calm and restrained way.
- Responds to challenges rationally, avoiding inappropriate emotion.
- Deals with difficult emotional issues and then moves on.
- Manages conflicting pressures and tensions.
- Maintains professional ethics when confronted with pressure from others.
- Copes with ambiguity and deals with uncertainty and frustration.
- Resists pressure to make quick decisions where consideration is needed.
- Remains focused and in control of situation.
- Makes and carries through decisions, even though they are unpopular, difficult or controversial.
- Stands firmly by a position when it is right to do so.
- Defends their staff from excessive criticisms from outside the team.

**Negative indicators**

- Gets easily upset, frustrated and annoyed.
- Panics and becomes agitated when problems arise.
- Walks away from confrontation when it would be more appropriate to get involved.
- Needs constant reassurance, support and supervision.
- Uses inappropriate physical force.

- Gets too emotionally involved in situations.

- Reacts inappropriately when faced with rude or abusive people.

- Deals with situations aggressively.

- Complains and whinges about problems rather than dealing with them.

- Gives in inappropriately when under pressure.

- Worries about making mistakes and avoids difficult situations wherever possible.

# Index

## Titles in the Practical Policing Skills series

Interactive Exercises for the Police Recruit
Assessment Process                                 ISBN: 9781844452491

Interview Exercises for the Police Recruit
Assessment Process                                 ISBN: 9781844454617

Law for Student Police Officers 2nd Ed             ISBN: 9781844452507

Passing the PCSO Recruit Assessment Process        ISBN: 9781846410598

Passing the Police Recruit Assessment Process      ISBN: 9781846410185

Practical Policing Skills for Student Officers
2nd Ed                                             ISBN: 9781846410529

Practical Skills for Police Community Support
Officers                                           ISBN: 9781846410406

Verbal and Numerical Reasoning Exercises for
the Police Recruit Assessment Process Process      ISBN: 9781844454624

Written Exercises for the Police Recruit
Assessment Process                                 ISBN: 9781844452668


To order, please contact our distributor: BEBC Distribution, Albion Close, Parkstone,
Poole, BH12 3LL. Telephone: 0845 230 9000, email: learningmatters@bebc.co.uk.
You can also find more information on each of these titles and our other learning
resources at www.learningmatters.co.uk.